Patrick Feury

TORE WRETMAN

THE SWEDISH SMÖRGÅS BORD

FORUM

CONTENTS

◁ FORUM ▷

©1983 BY TORE WRETMAN
TRANSLATION CLARE JAMES
REVISION AND EDITING SIGNE ROLF
TYPOGRAPHICAL DESIGN PAUL EKLUND
PHOTOGRAPHS JAN BENGTSSON
TYPESETTING BOKSTAVEN AB, GÖTEBORG
PRINTED IN SWEDEN BY BOKTRYCK AB, HELSINGBORG 1983
ISBN 91-37-08251-5

INTRODUCTION

THE SMÖRGÅSBORD (literally, "open-sandwich table") is not uniquely Swedish. The Russians have *zakuski*, the Danes have their *kolde bord*, and the French have *hors d'œuvre*. But none of these measures up to the Swedish smörgåsbord in composition, profusion of dishes, close association with ancient cooking traditions or importance to the cuisine of the country concerned.

A considerable number of the dishes found on a replete smörgåsbord originated in the impoverished Sweden of the early nineteenth century. A remarkable development has taken place: foods which in olden times (and one need go back no further than a century) constituted the everyday dietary staples of the poor are now regarded as the country's true delicacies. Of these, many have become luxuries, owing to the high prices commanded by their raw ingredients.

The manner in which food is prepared, or rather conserved, is also a survival from the past, although for the most part methods have become more refined. It is also worth stressing that the majority of dishes on the Swedish smörgåsbord are excellent served on their own, both for everyday meals and on festive occasions.

Sweden has a long coastline and, moreover, an abundance of rivers and lakes. There is water varying in salt content and temperature, which in turn means a rich variety of fish species. As a result, fish has not surprisingly been an important food since prehistoric times. Supplies of the main varieties of fish – herring and salmon – were irregular, and methods such as salting, drying and smoking were therefore used in the olden days to conserve food for longer periods. In northern Sweden, too, the ice which covers lakes and rivers for half of every year makes fishing an arduous task during those months.

Marinating is one of the oldest curing methods. The Swedish word for it, "gravning", comes from the word "begrava", which means "bury". Formerly, salt was expensive, so fish was salted sparingly and then buried in the ground in order to preserve it from the deleterious effects of atmospheric oxygen. By this means, fermentation was also caused. Fermentation is another extremely old Swedish method of preserving food.

The modern smörgåsbord's marinated salmon, mackerel or herring have, needless to say, never been buried in the ground. Nor have they undergone fermentation. Nowadays, the word "gravning" denotes "sugar-salting": the fish is rubbed with a mixture of salt, sugar and seasoning, and left to mature for a day or two in the refrigerator. It is then ready to serve with no further preparation, accompanied by its own special "gravlax" sauce, a sweet-sour mustard dressing.

Herring of various kinds have throughout history been caught in large numbers around the coasts of Sweden. But the finest large herring for salting is caught in the coastal waters of Iceland and Norway. It is a big, plump herring well suited to pickling of one kind and another. Large herring are also caught off the west coast of Sweden – in the Kattegat – and in the North Sea; here, too, are various kinds of small herring, including sprats, used for the specifically Swedish canned variety of anchovies. Off the southernmost Baltic coast, with a northern limit at the city of Kalmar on the east coast, yet another variety of herring is caught, namely "strömming" or Baltic herring. The further north you go, the smaller this fish becomes, owing to the fact that the waters of the Gulf of Bothnia (the northern part of the Baltic) are colder and less salty than the rest of the Baltic. Smoked Baltic herring is called "böckling", and was probably named after the German who originated it, sometime in the 15th century.

Although the Baltic herring is one particular species, other types of small herring can replace it in the recipes given here.

One of the main features distinguishing the Swedish smörgåsbord from its foreign counterparts is its large proportion of dishes based on salt and Baltic herring. A proper smörgåsbord without pickled herring is unthinkable.

Salt herring is used in many ways. Swedes often eat it just as it is, after soaking it in water for several hours to get rid of most of the salt. Then it is served with piping-hot new potatoes boiled with dill, and accompanied by sour cream and chives. The next stage in the preparation is to place the soaked, filleted herring in a sweet-and-sour solution of white spirit vinegar, sugar and seasoning. The varying flavors and characteristics of the many herring dishes depend on the particular herbs and spices used in their preparation.

The custom of laying out all sorts of food on the table at once is supposed to have begun in Sweden sometime in the 16th century. The smörgåsbord in its present form originated in the "brännvin table" of the 18th century ("brännvin", literally "fiery wine", is Swedish schnapps). This was the first course of a banquet, and would be laid on a separate table in a corner of the dining room, or an adjoining room, as a buffet consisting of various kinds of brännvin, herring, homemade pickled anchovies, bread and strongly flavored cheese. Guests would partake of the brännvin table standing up, before taking their seats around the dining table for the banquet proper.

More and more dishes were added to this brännvin table, and in due course it developed into the gigantic smörgåsbord which reached its zenith – for both home and restaurant cooking – in the 19th century.

At that time the great brännvin urn, which was large enough to hold containers for several sorts of brännvin, had pride of place in the center of the table. It was just a matter of turning the faucet for the fiery liquor one desired as an aperitif. Around the urn, hot and cold delicacies were set out. The smörgåsbord was still "only" the introduction to a meal.

Today, eating habits have changed: the smörgåsbord constitutes the whole meal, and yet the full appreciation of the smörgåsbord is – thanks to the many delicious specialities – something of an art. In Swedish homes, the smörgåsbord has shrunk drastically – except at Christmas. Then a magnificent Christmas table is the rule for the great majority of Swedes: the smörgåsbord's delicacies are complemented, or in some cases replaced, by some typical old-fashioned Christmas dishes such as mustard-glazed Yule ham, headcheese and a few varieties of sausage.

Around the Swedish smörgåsbord, the air is fragrant

with the smells of chopped onion and dill, fresh boiled potatoes with dill, ground pepper and cloves, hot dishes consisting of anchovies, potatoes and onions baked in the oven, spiced cheeses and vinegar preserves.

It is also a feast for the eye, with its glorious range of colors. Glassblower's herring, for example, has silvery chunks of herring, bright slivers of carrot, onion rings and coal-black allspice. Other herring preserves are made with the accompaniments chopped into strips of green, white and yellow. The translucent green of pickled gherkins, the crimson of beets, the delicate shell-pink of marinated salmon, the oscillations of pork in aspic... Artistic arrangements and elaborate decorations are quite superfluous.

The Swede drinks beer and brännvin with his smörgåsbord – there is no question of anything else, although of course for the teetotaler and motorist milk and water may be substituted. Swedish traffic laws are strict, so sobriety at the steering wheel is a must.

Brännvin is distilled in the same way as Russian vodka. It varies, however, greatly in flavor: from an unflavored vodka to one strongly flavored with different spices and herbs. One of the most popular is "Skåne", an aquavit originally from the southern province of that name, lightly flavored with caraway seeds. There are at least twenty flavored varieties, which are called aquavit (water of life), while the uncolored and unspiced variety is called "Absolut Renat Brännvin" or "Absolute Vodka". This is the purest alcohol, made from either barley or potatoes.

There is a whole ritual connected with drinking brännvin in Sweden. Brännvin is called "snaps" when it is imbibed with food. It is de rigueur to raise glasses for a mutual "Skål" before you start drinking this snaps. What the Swede likes best is a song with the snaps. The first glassful is called "helan" ("the whole one"), the second "halvan" ("the half") and the third "tersen" ("the tierce"). The first has its own song, as does the second. There are countless more or less witty snaps-song variations. Snaps-drinking at Christmas is accompanied by its own specific song, "Hej tomtegubbar..." ("Hi elfmen..."). Otherwise, the best-known is "Helan går", here given in Swedish and in a humorous "English" transcription:

Helan går
sjung hopp fallerallanlallanlej.
Helan går
sjung hopp fallerallanlej.
Och han som inte Helan tar
han heller inte Halvan får.
Helan går

—

sjung hopp fallerallanlej!

Hell and gore
Chung Hop father Allan Allan ley.
Hell and gore
Chung Hop father Allan ley.
Oh handsome in the hell and tar
and hell are in the half and four.
Hell and gore

—

Chung Hop father Allan ley!

Let us now, in a devotional spirit, approach the resplendent dinner table in the order dictated by tradition and good sense, in order not to miss any of its delights.

The first and most important rule of all is to take your time: you should never be in a hurry when dealing with the smörgåsbord. You can go back to the table again and again. You change your plate from time to time, when the preceding dish leaves flavors and vestiges which do not harmonize with the next. You should make at least five – preferably six or more – visits before you are through with the meal. It is execrable to overload your plate with an indiscriminate assortment.

Your first trip should be devoted to the herring and the cheese. For foreigners, one of the hardest of all our remarkable Swedish eating habits to understand is that of eating cheese as a first course and, what is more, of combining it with herring and its sundry accompaniments. It should be remembered that cheese in this context means the hard type of cheese typically used for open sandwiches, a product of Swedish peasant life. Soft dessert cheeses do not belong on the smörgåsbord.

Crispbread, thin unleavened bread and ryemeal loaves are typically Swedish, and go well with both the herring and the cheese. At Christmas, we eat rye bread flavored with wort (an infusion of malt which, when fermented, makes beer) with the smörgåsbord.

The second round consists of other fish dishes, among which salmon is paramount. Then there is eel, prepared in various ways. Unshelled prawns are included here, although they really require a visit of their own – the shelling process definitely necessitates its own plate.

In the third round, you sample the meats. Among these are specialities such as dried leg of mutton and smoked reindeer, sausages, headcheese, joints, poultry and jellied meats. With these are salads and tasty extras such as gherkins and pickled beetroot, cucumber preserve, cucumber pickle and perhaps green tomato pickle as well.

The fourth time round, we have reached what is called "småvarmt" (the hot buffet) in Swedish: light, dainty dishes such as salt and fresh fish, meat, eggs and vegetables. At least one salty dish, one very mild and one that is somewhat substantial should be included.

When you have come this far in sampling the temptations of the smörgåsbord, you should take your time. Take small portions, and savor them at your leisure, sitting down.

The fifth visit to the table is the final, satisfying one that rounds off your meal. After all the salty, smoked and rich food, the palate needs something sweet and something refreshing. The refreshment is perhaps best of all provided by a fruit salad, made of pure fresh fruit; but a Swedish apple pie goes down pretty well too. Sweetness may be supplied by some cookies with the coffee, which is the ultimate thing needed to complete your enjoyment of the Swedish smörgåsbord.

And now, my friends, the table is laid and we are ready for the party to begin.

The photographs of the smörgåsbord in this book were taken at the Operakällaren restaurant in Stockholm. The table is laid in accordance with the principle of five "rounds" or courses.

1. Gentleman's savory.
2. Sour cream.
3. Chopped onions.
4. River trout roe.
5. Marinated smoked Baltic herring.
6. Black olives.
7. Green olives.
8. Pickled onions.
9. Matjes herring.
10. Baltic herring marinated in mustard dressing.
11. Pickled Baltic herring.
12. Baltic herring with Swedish caviar.
13. Pickled salt herring.
14. Spiced herring.
15. Glassblower's herring.
16. Moja herring, matjes herring in Rhode Island sauce.
17. Poached Baltic herring.

The smoked Baltic herring, Baltic herring with Swedish caviar and poached Baltic herring may also be eaten in the second round. The olives and pickled onions perhaps go best with the cold meat in the third round.

1. Poached salmon.
2. Rhode Island sauce.
3. Mayonnaise.
4. Smoked salmon.
5. Cheeses.
6. Melon.
7. Parma ham.
8. Crispbread.
9. Spring salad.
10. Dill-cured salmon salad.
11. Prawn salad.
12. Prawns.
13. Moja salad, a prawn salad with Rhode Island sauce.

14. Poached salmon fins.
15. Prawn eggs.
16. Bleak roe eggs.
17. Tomato salad.
18. Marinated asparagus.

The cheese and crispbread are preferably eaten with the herring in the first round, in accordance with Swedish tradition. The Parma ham may also form part of the third round, with other cold cuts.

1. Mimosa salad.   5. Chicken liver mousse.   9. Boiled ham.
2. Chicken salad.   6. Smoked eel.   10. Boiled tongue.
3. Beef salad.   7. Roast beef.   11. Salt leg of beef.
4. Pigeon pâté.   8. Smoked lamb.   12. Apple purée.

13. Pickled cucumber.
14. Pickles.
15. Pickled beets.
16. Cumberland sauce.

17. Sausages of various kinds.
18. Pâtés.
19. Smoked reindeer.

The smoked eel
may also be eaten in
the second round.

1. Fried chipolata sausages.
2. Meatballs.
3. Shellfish au gratin.
4. Boiled potatoes.
5. Herring au gratin.
6. Jansson's temptation.
7. Gravy.
8. Omelet.
9. Swedish beefburgers.
10. Tomato sauce.

Boiled potatoes go best
with the herring in
the first round.

1. Fresh fruit.
2. Fruit salad.
3. King Oscar's cake.

HERRING IS THE FIRST and foremost dish on the Swedish smörgåsbord. It is herring which, more than anything else, bestows character on this veritable bonanza of food. There cannot be a smörgåsbord without it: many other dishes can be omitted, but not herring.

At the same time, it serves to remind us of the past. The great herring fisheries of the North Sea and its coasts have throughout history been of crucial importance. In medieval times they saved many from death by starvation.

Nowadays we eat herring in all its forms mainly because it tastes good, which is more than one can say for some medieval household staples.

All the salted fish appears in the first round: everything from the original version, salt herring with chives and sour cream, to spicy, pickled varieties in which the fish has lain for weeks in salt, sugar and spices in order to ripen to a full, rich flavor.

The first round also includes Baltic herring, a diminutive cousin of the common herring, which can be pickled or marinated. Then there are Swedish anchovies, served either whole, straight from the can, or in small savory side dishes, in which the particular Swedish sauce it is preserved in is an important seasoning element. Another element is Swedish caviar, of which there are two kinds. One is made of cod's roe with sugar and salt added and sometimes also smoked. The other is fresh, slightly salted bleak roe with its golden yellow granules. The bleak is a small fish from the extreme north of Scandinavia, living in the lakes and the gulf of Bothnia. Bleak roe should not be confused with artificially black- or red-colored canned lumpfish roe from Germany and Denmark. The variety used for the smörgåsbord is salted and canned.

Cheese is important. There should be mature Västerbotten (a plain, strong cheese somewhat resembling Cheddar) or equivalent, some form of spiced cheese with whole caraway seeds in it, and perhaps a genuine whey-cheese made of goat's milk whey. Another welcome addition is the Swedish version of potted cheese.

Last but not least, bread should accompany every round, and forms the correct background to the various dishes. There should be crispbread and thin, unleavened bread; soft rye bread and black ryemeal bread. Butter goes without saying – as do hot, preferably new, boiled potatoes with dill.

SOS – Save Our Souls – may perhaps have a double meaning, when found on a Swedish restaurant menu. But it stands primarily for "Smör, Ost och Sill", which means just a small herring buffet.

First-round Dishes

Salt Herring with Chives and Sour Cream
Matjes Herring
Pickled Salt Herring
Aquavit Herring
Glassblower's Herring
Mustard Herring
Fiddler's Herring
Herring Salad
Amanda Svensson's Spiced Herring
Marinated Baltic Herring
Baltic Herring Marinated in Mustard Dressing
Spiced Rollmops
Baltic Herring with Onion
Herring, Russian Style
Pickled Baltic Herring
Swedish Anchovies
Swedish Anchovies, Grandma-style
Bird's Nest
Gentleman's Savory
Bleak Roe with Sour Cream
Swedish Caviar Mound
Spiced Roe
Assorted Cheeses
Swedish Potted Cheese
Assorted Swedish Breads
Butter
Freshly Boiled Potatoes with Dill

SPICKEN SILL MED GRÄSLÖK OCH SUR GRÄDDE

The word "spicken" is of ancient Swedish origin, and refers to an equally antiquated preserving method. In olden times, fish and meat were preserved by stretching them out with the aid of wooden sticks ("spiker" in old Swedish) and then drying and salting them. Nowadays, "spicken" in the fish context means simply that it is salted; when applied to ham or sausages, it means that the meat is sun-dried and salted, sometimes smoked as well.

Salt herring is raw, but nevertheless ready to eat after draining. Swedes eat it often and gladly, particularly in summer, for lunch or dinner, with dill-flavored potatoes, chives and sour cream. It is simple to prepare.

Clean the salted herring, and soak it in water for about 6 hours. Rinse and dry it well, pull off the skin and cut it diagonally in pieces about 3 cm (an inch) thick. Lay it on a serving dish in the shape of the whole fish. Garnish with sprigs of dill. Place bowls of chopped chives and half-whipped sour cream nearby.

MATJES HERRING

MATJESSILL

This is served in the same manner as salt herring, with chives and sour cream, but it need not be drained first. The word "matjes" is Dutch, and means "maiden". The herring is caught immediately before reaching sexual maturity, when it is extra plump, and then preserved in sugar and salt.

INLAGD SILL

Pickled salt herring is dear to the Swede's heart, and never absent from a real Swedish smörgåsbord. Preparation methods are numerous and highly idiosyncratic. This version is well seasoned and tasty.

2 large salt herrings

FOR THE PICKLE:
1 ½ dl (¾ cup) white spirit
  vinegar (12%)
1 ½ dl (¾ cup) water
½ dl (¼ cup) sugar
1 chopped onion
¼ tsp thyme
½ tsp crushed allspice
½ tsp crushed white peppercorns
2 bay leaves

FOR THE GARNISH:
1 red onion, sliced thinly
2 tbsp coarsely chopped parsley
½ tsp crushed allspice

Clean, skin and fillet the fish. Take care to remove all small bones. Soak the fillets in cold water to cover for about 5 hours. Mix all the ingredients for the dressing in a saucepan and bring to the boil, stirring in order to dissolve the sugar. Allow it to boil for several minutes, then leave it to cool.

Dry the drained fillets well and cut them crosswise in bite-sized pieces. Arrange them in a broad, flat-bottomed bowl. Pour the cold dressing on top. Garnish with rows of red onion and parsley, with a thin band of crushed allspice in the middle.

This herring dish, like others, is an excellent lunch dish if accompanied by piping-hot, freshly boiled new potatoes seasoned with dill.

4 herring fillets, drained
4 ½ dl (2 cups) water
2 dl (¾ cup) wine vinegar
2 dl (¾ cup) sugar
25 whole allspice
20 white peppercorns
2 whole cloves
4 bay leaves
¼ tsp caraway seeds
¼ tsp aniseed
1 piece of lemon rind
5 cl (¼ cup) aquavit

FOR THE GARNISH:
½ apple cut into matchstick-thin strips
½ peeled lemon in thin slices
1 tsp crushed juniper berries
1 small carrot in matchstick-thin strips
1 small onion in slices
3 sprigs of dill

Bring to a boil the water with the vinegar, sugar, pepper, cloves, bay leaves, caraway seeds, aniseed and lemon peel. . Stir until the sugar is dissolved and the solution is clear. Leave to cool.

Cut the dry herring fillets diagonally into 2 cm (¾ inch) pieces and lay them in a flat-bottomed bowl in such a way as to look whole. Pour the cold dressing on top and leave overnight in the refrigerator.

Garnish with apple, lemon, juniper berries, carrot strips, onion and dill arranged in rows. Pour the aquavit over the herring.

GLASMÄSTARSILL

This version of marinated herring ought to remain in the refrigerator for several days, so that the blend of flavors in the dressing can impart full aroma and maturity to the herring. Then it is magnificent.

2 large salt herrings
1 carrot
2 red onions
1 large leek
1 ½ dl (¾ cup) white spirit
 vinegar (12%)
1 ½ dl (¾ cup) water
1 dl (½ cup) sugar
4 bay leaves
1 tsp crushed white peppercorns
2 tsp crushed allspice
2 tsp mustard seeds
10 cloves
1 piece of horseradish
2 tbsp chopped dill
2 tbsp chopped parsley

Clean the herring, removing scales and fins but leaving the skin. Soak overnight in cold water to cover.

Cut the carrot, onion and leek in thin slices.

Mix the spirit vinegar, water and sugar in a saucepan. Add half of the sliced vegetables and half the seasoning. Bring to the boil and simmer for about 10 minutes. Leave to cool. Sieve, then discard the vegetables.

Rinse the herring and dry it thoroughly. Cut it diagonally in slices about 3 cm (an inch) thick. Place it in a glass jar or pot with the remainder of the sliced vegetables, seasoning, diced horseradish, dill and parsley, adding the vegetables last. Pour the dressing in and use a light weight, e.g. a piece of carrot, to keep the herring submerged.

Leave in the refrigerator for 4–5 days. To serve, sprinkle with chopped dill and parsley.

SENAPSSILL

2 large salt herrings
½ dl (¼ cup) white spirit
  vinegar (12%)
1 ½ dl (¾ cup) water
1 tbsp sugar
1 tbsp salt

FOR THE DRESSING:
¼ dl (⅛ cup) wine vinegar
½ dl (¼ cup) thick cream
1 tbsp dark, unsweetened
  French mustard
1 tbsp Swedish mustard
½ tsp ground white pepper
1 dl (½ cup) oil
2 tbsp chopped dill

FOR THE GARNISH:
chopped dill
1 hard-boiled egg

Clean and fillet the herring. Take great care to remove as many small bones as possible (using a pair of tweezers).

Put the fillets to soak in water to cover for about 6 hours. Bring to a boil the spirit vinegar, water, sugar and salt. Leave to cool. Put the fillets to stand in the refrigerator, in the dressing, for several hours.

Whisk together the wine vinegar, mustard, cream and white pepper for the dressing. Add the oil, at first drop by drop and then in a fine stream, whisking continuously. Mix in the finely chopped dill.

Dry the herring fillets with kitchen paper. Cut them diagonally in bite-sized pieces.

Pour a layer of dressing into a deep dish; arrange the fillets – keeping the shape of the whole fish – on top, and then pour the rest of the dressing over them.

Garnish with chopped dill and chopped hard-boiled egg in rows on top of the herring.

1 large salt herring
2 tbsp sugar
2 dl (¾ cup) sour cream
2 hard-boiled eggs
2 tbsp chopped chives
2 tbsp chopped parsley

Clean and fillet the herring. Remove as many small bones as possible. Soak the fillets in water to cover for 5–6 hours.

Dry the fillets well. Cut them crosswise in bite-sized pieces. Arrange on a serving dish with a raised edge in such a way that they look whole.

Sprinkle sugar on top, and chill for a few hours. Cover the herring with sour cream and garnish with diagonal bands of chopped egg white, chopped chives, chopped yolk and chopped parsley.

Fiddler's herring makes an excellent luncheon dish, served with freshly boiled new potatoes.

Herring Salad

SILLSALLAD

1 large salt herring
3 cold boiled potatoes
4 large pickled beets
1 large cooking apple
2 pickled gherkins
1 dl (½ cup) leftover boiled
    or fried beef
1 onion
3–4 tbsp pickled beet juice
¼ tsp freshly ground white pepper
(½ tsp salt)
½ dl (¼ cup) whipped cream

FOR THE GARNISH:
cold hard-boiled eggs

Clean the fish, fillet it and remove the skin. Take great care to remove all small bones. Soak the fillets in cold water to cover overnight.

Finely dice the herring, potatoes, beets, apple, gherkins and beef; finely chop the onion.

Mix all the ingredients well, and add the pickled beet juice. Add freshly ground white pepper and perhaps a little salt, to taste. A little cream should also, preferably, be added.

Pack the salad into a mold which has been rinsed in cold water, and chill for 3–4 hours. Unmold.

Chop the hard-boiled eggs, keeping the yolks and whites separate. Garnish the salad with these, in alternate bands of yellow and white.

AMANDA SVENSSONS KRYDDSILL

Spiced herring is above all a speciality of Skåne (Scania), Sweden's southernmost province, the long coasts of which provide a particular type of small herring which is especially well suited to this spicy dressing.

Skåne is also Sweden's most fertile province, with a cuisine somewhat distinct from that of the rest of the country.

> 40 absolutely fresh small
>   herrings (approx. 2 kg, 4 ½ lb)
> 3 dl (1 ¼ cups) white spirit
>   vinegar (12%)
> 6 dl (2 ½ cups) water
> 1 tbsp salt
> 250 g (1 cup) non-iodized salt
> 400 g (1 ½ cups) sugar
> 5 coarsely crushed bay leaves
> 2 tsp crushed white peppercorns
> 2 tsp crushed allspice
> 5 g hops
> 5 g sandalwood
> 20 cloves
> 12 g saltpeter

Remove the head and intestines from the herring, then lay it in a mixture of spirit vinegar, water and salt and chill for a day or so.

Mix the salt, sugar and all the seasoning except the saltpeter. Cover the bottom of a pot or glass jar with the mixture, then place on top a layer of well drained herring, with their backs uppermost.

Sprinkle the seasoning blend on top again. Continue arranging the fish and seasoning in alternate layers, finishing with a layer of seasoning. Store in the refrigerator for about three weeks before serving.

1 kg (2 lb) cleaned, filleted
(1 ½ kg or 3 lb whole) Baltic herring

MARINADE 1:
5 dl (2 cups) water
1 dl (⅜ cup) white spirit
vinegar (12%)
1 dl (⅜ cup) salt

MARINADE 2:
5 dl (2 cups) water
1 dl (⅜ cup) sugar
1 dl (⅜ cup) white spirit
vinegar (12%)
10 crushed white peppercorns
½ dl (¼ cup) oil

FOR THE GARNISH:
1 bunch of dill

Clean, bone and rinse the herring. If possible, remove the skin. Soak the fillets in the first marinade (water, spirit vinegar and salt) for 3–4 hours.

Remove and drain the herring.

Mix the ingredients for the second marinade, and pour this over the herring fillets so that they are well covered. Leave overnight in a cool place.

Sprinkle finely chopped dill on top before serving.

SENAPSGRAVAD STRÖMMING

1 kg (2 lb) Baltic herring
approx. 1 ½ dl (⅝ cup) milk
1 ½ tsp salt

FOR THE MUSTARD DRESSING:
2 tsp mustard powder
1 tbsp sugar
1 dl (½ cup) oil
½ tbsp salt
¼ tsp crushed white pepper
½ dl (¼ cup) white spirit
    vinegar (12%)
½ dl (¼ cup) water
1 large bunch of dill

Clean, bone and fillet the herring. Soak the fillets for a few hours in the milk, in which the salt has been dissolved.

Mix the mustard powder, sugar, oil, salt, white pepper, spirit vinegar and water. Chop the dill and stir in half of it; lay the fillets on top and then sprinkle the other half over them. Chill for several hours before serving.

A good luncheon dish, served with freshly boiled dill potatoes.

600 g (1 ½ lb) cleaned, boned
  Baltic herring
3 tsp salt
½ dl (¼ cup) water
2 tbsp crushed allspice
1 large chopped red onion
  (approx. ½ dl, ⅝ cup)

For the dressing:
¾ dl (⅜ cup) white spirit
  vinegar (12%)
¾ dl (⅜ cup) water
¾ dl (⅜ cup) sugar

Salt the Baltic herring fillets and roll them up. Lay them in a wide saucepan and pour the water on top. Bring to a boil gently, and simmer them under cover for 8–10 minutes.

Discard the water. Cover the herring with crushed allspice. Leave to cool, then sprinkle the chopped onion over the fish. Make a dressing of the spirit vinegar, water and sugar, and pour it on top.

Chill for 24 hours before serving, accompanied by freshly boiled potatoes with dill.

1 kg (2 lb) fresh Baltic herrings

FOR THE MARINADE:
2 dl (¾ cup) white spirit
vinegar (12%)
2 dl (¾ cup) water

FOR THE DRESSING:
½ dl (¼ cup) salt
1 dl (½ cup) sugar
10 cloves
2 coarsely crushed bay leaves
1 tsp crushed white pepper
1 tbsp crushed allspice
2 large onions

Clean and rinse the herring, but do not remove the backbones. Mix the spirit vinegar and water, and soak the herring in this mixture overnight, in a cool place.

Mix the salt, sugar and seasoning. Cut the onion in thin slices. Put a layer of the seasoning mixture in the bottom of a jar or pot, followed by a layer of herring and one of onion. Continue alternating the layers in this way, finishing with a layer of onion.

Cover with a lid or plastic film, and chill for three days before serving.

Herring, Russian Style

It is worth preparing a large batch of this herring: the longer you keep it, the better it gets, and it stays fresh for about four months.

> 4–5 fresh herrings, with heads removed
> approx. 1 liter (2 pints) strong, cold tea
> 5 dl (2 cups) milk
> 1 dl (½ cup) sugar
> 150 g (1 cup) non-iodized salt
> ½ tbsp ground ginger
> 5 g Spanish hops
> 2 tsp crushed allspice
> 2 tsp crushed white pepper
> 5 crushed bay leaves
> 1 stick cinnamon, coarsely crushed
> 2 ½ dl (1 cup) oil
> 2 ½ dl (1 cup) wine vinegar

The herring should be cleaned, but not rinsed. Put it to soak in the strong, cold tea for about 12 hours, and then discard the tea and pour the milk over the herring. Stir, then put aside overnight (about 12 hours).

Mix the sugar, salt and other seasoning, and shake the oil and vinegar together.

Spread a little of the seasoning mixture on the bottom of a glass jar or pot. Place on top a layer of herring, with backs uppermost, and then sprinkle another layer of seasoning over these. Pour a little of the oil mixture on top, and continue alternating layers in this way. Finish with a layer of seasoning and oil mixture.

Chill for at least a fortnight before serving to allow the herring to mature.

20 Baltic herrings, dipped in egg,
    coated in breadcrumbs and fried,
    still hot
6 crushed allspice
6 crushed white peppercorns

FOR THE DRESSING:
1 sliced onion
1 ½ dl (¾ cup) white spirit
    vinegar (12%)
1 ½ dl (¾ cup) water
1 tbsp sugar or syrup

FOR THE GARNISH:
a few sprigs of dill
½ sliced red onion

Mix the ingredients for the dressing. Bring to the boil and
simmer for 10 minutes, then leave to cool. Place the herring in
layers in a flat-bottomed, steep-sided bowl, seasoning each
layer as you go. Pour the cold dressing over the hot herring.
Decorate with sprigs of dill and sliced red onion.

    Chill the herring for several hours before serving.

The Swedish word "ansjovis" is not the name of a fish, but rather of a method of preserving herring. The herring used for "ansjovis" is, however, a close relative of the genuine anchovy (which is to be found chiefly in the Mediterranean, and off the Atlantic coasts of Europe as far north as Bergen in Norway). This cousin of the anchovy which is used for the Swedish "ansjovis" is called a sprat *(Sprattus sprattus)*. The sprats which are thus preserved are caught primarily off the coast of Bohuslän, a county in the west of Sweden, and processed at the canning factories there. Sprats are caught between the end of September and sometime in January. In the first few weeks of the season, this herring is extra plump and good to eat.

For preserving, the sprat is rubbed with a mixture of sugar, salt and spices such as cinnamon, ginger, pepper, cardamom and sandalwood. Every factory has its own secret recipe.

The pickled sprats are left to ripen for several weeks in the cans before they are sold. The best, caught early, are just at the right stage of maturity by Christmas, and are also sold as Christmas ansjovis.

Maturity may be discerned from the easy separation of the flesh from the backbone during cleaning.

Ansjovis are available both whole and in fillets, free of bones and skin, in cans; the former taste best.

Several dishes on the Swedish smörgåsbord are based on ansjovis. It may also be eaten just as it is – after removing the skin and bones, of course.

12–15 sprat fillets
3 tbsp oil
1 tbsp wine vinegar
3 tbsp tomato purée
1 tsp mustard
a little salt
a little ground black pepper

FOR THE GARNISH:
2 tbsp chopped chives
2 hard-boiled egg yolks, chopped
2 hard-boiled egg whites, chopped
2 tbsp chopped parsley

Lay the sprat fillets on a serving dish. Mix the oil, vinegar, tomato purée, mustard, salt and pepper thoroughly. Distribute the mixture evenly over the fillets.

Put the finely chopped chives, parsley, egg yolks and whites in alternating bands on top of the fish, allowing the red dressing to show through.

BIRD'S NEST

FÅGELBO

4 raw egg yolks
16 finely chopped sprat fillets
2–3 tbsp finely chopped onion
3–4 tbsp finely chopped capers
3–4 tbsp finely chopped pickled beets
3–4 tbsp finely chopped parsley
3–4 tbsp finely chopped chives

Place all the ingredients except the parsley in a circle of small heaps on a dish, so as to obtain a pleasing color distribution. Put the parsley in the middle, and carefully lay the yolks – each in its half-shell – on the bed of parsley.

Each guest helps himself to a little from each pile and one of the egg yolks, and then mixes it all together on his own plate.

GENTLEMAN'S SAVORY

GUBBRÖRA

4–5 hard-boiled eggs
2 raw egg yolks
2 tbsp salted Swedish caviar
4–5 sprat fillets
2 tbsp finely chopped dill
2 tbsp finely chopped parsley
2 tbsp finely chopped chives

Make a purée of the hard-boiled eggs and raw yolks. Mix with the salted Swedish caviar and the finely chopped sprat fillets. Finally, blend in the finely chopped herbs. Serve chilled.

Roe – from many different fish – is a much-appreciated delicacy in Sweden, eaten both on festive and on everyday occasions. Bleak roe comes at the very top of the culinary list. The bleak is a small fish caught in the northern part of the Gulf of Bothnia and in lakes north of the Arctic Circle. Its roe is eaten raw, lightly salted and served with sour cream or *crème fraîche* and very finely chopped onion or chives, preferably on a small piece of buttered toast. Bleak roe with baked potatoes and the above accompaniments is a prized first course. Roe from salted trout and lake trout is eaten in the same way.

What the Swedes call "caviar" is cod's roe, which has had sugar and salt added and sometimes been smoked, as well as blended with oil to a greater or lesser extent. It is usually sold in tubes, and is a popular sandwich topping for everyday use. Swedes on long trips abroad usually miss the caviar open sandwich acutely.

Highly salted, smoked caviar is available in cans. It is used mainly in diluted form, as for example in the recipe for Swedish caviar mound (see p. 37).

Bleak roe is often sold deep-frozen in Sweden: it has then been cleaned and lightly salted directly after the fish has been caught. Neither the taste nor the consistency of bleak roe suffers from being deep-frozen.

Bleak Roe with Sour Cream

LÖJROM MED GRÄDDFIL

On the smörgåsbord, lightly salted bleak roe is served with individual bowls of sour cream, chopped chives, chopped red onion and lemon wedges.

Swedish Caviar Mound

KAVIARTOPP

2 ½ dl (1 cup) whipping cream
1–2 tbsp salted Swedish caviar
or 2–3 tbsp smoked Swedish
  caviar (sold in tubes)
1 finely chopped onion
a few dill sprigs for garnishing

Whip the cream until it is stiff, then mix in the salted caviar. Taste as you go along, so that the mixture does not become too salty.

Pile up the caviar cream in the middle of a round serving dish. Put a circle of finely chopped onion around the base and some flowering heads of dill on top of the mound.

This caviar cream tastes excellent on Swedish crispbread.

Spiced Roe

KRYDDAD ROM

Fish roe (you have pike, turbot, bleak, whitefish, lumpfish or cod to choose from) is treatcd as follows.

First the roe is cleaned thoroughly to remove membranes and traces of blood. To 3 dl (1 cup) of cleaned roe, use ¼ teaspoonful of newly ground white pepper, 1 tablespoonful of lemon juice and approx. ½ tsp salt. Mix all these thoroughly with the roe and work them in; then pack the mixture into a glass jar and chill for 12–24 hours. You can also work in a parboiled, finely chopped red onion. But, for the guests' sake, it is better to serve chopped red onion separately, like the sour cream.

Surplus roe may be deep-frozen, but not for long periods. Moreover, the frozen roe must not contain onion, since this has a detrimental effect on the flavor when the two are frozen together.

The "smörgås" or open sandwich – bread and butter with some kind of topping – is a particularly popular form of sandwich eaten by Swedes at all times of the day.

A slice of cheese is by far the commonest sandwich topping, and the cheeses used are without exception hard. Formerly, hard cheeses of various kinds were home-made in various parts of the country, and varied widely in character. The best-known – and best – of these cheeses are: *Västerbottensost*, a strong, well aged and somewhat sharp porous cheese made in the northernmost part of Sweden; *Prästost*, which is closely related to Västerbottensost, but somewhat milder; *Kryddost*, a porous cheese containing an abundance of whole caraway seeds; *Herrgårdsost*, a Swiss-type cheese, mild but (when sufficiently aged) tasty, as is *Greveost*, which has a somewhat stronger flavor; and *Mesost*, which is not in fact a cheese at all but is made of the whey obtained when making cow's and goat's milk cheeses.

These cheeses are nowadays invariably factory-produced.

Soft dessert cheeses such as Gorgonzola and Roquefort do not belong on the Swedish smörgåsbord.

SWEDISH POTTED CHEESE

POTKES

Swedish potted cheese ("Potkes") is a splendid way of using up the leftovers of good hard cheeses. The cheese is grated, or pounded to pieces in a mortar, and then sieved through a strainer or colander. Next, a little cream is stirred in, followed by butter. A little brandy or brännvin should then be added, and the mixture worked until it is a smooth dough. Finally, season with salt, ground white pepper, finely crushed caraway seeds, cloves, a pinch of ground cinnamon and perhaps some cayenne pepper. If a dark potted cheese is desired, a few drops of genuine Japanese soya sauce may be worked in. The cheese is then packed into small china dishes and left to mature for several days in the refrigerator.

CRISPBREAD

KNÄCKEBRÖD

Crispbread is an ancient Swedish speciality and an integral part of the smörgåsbord. Originally, it was always a coarse, wholemeal rye bread owing its dryness and durability to the high temperature at which it was baked. It was made in the form of large, thin, round cakes with holes in the centers; a pole threaded through these holes and suspended from the ceiling above a wooden stove was the traditional countryfolk's method of storing it. Nowadays, crispbread of many different kinds is available – varying in the proportions of finely ground flour used, including wheat but principally of the wholemeal variety. Some types are very crisp and easy to chew, while others offer considerably more resistance to the teeth. Crispbread is always unsweetened, and often machine-cut in portions.

In recent years, Swedish crispbread has spread to various parts of the world, together with closely related Norwegian and Finnish varieties.

TUNNBRÖD

Tunnbröd, a kind of soft, thin, unleavened bread, is another Swedish speciality, from the northernmost part of the country. It is baked in special ovens, originally in the form of extremely large and thin cakes requiring great dexterity to handle. Barley meal and potatoes were the ingredients used. Here, too, technology has ousted manual work, and most tunnbröd nowadays is machine-cut.

SOFT BREAD

A couple of varieties of soft bread – for example, the dark bread made of boiled ryemeal – complement the hard bread, as does ordinary Swedish rye bread and, at Christmas, "vörtlimpa" or wort-flavored rye bread (see p. 126).

Here is a classic recipe for "ring cakes".

RING CAKES

HÅLKAKOR

50 g (2 oz) fresh yeast
5 dl (2 ½ cups) milk
approx. 4 tbsp butter, margarine or lard
1 tsp salt
½ dl (¼ cup) syrup
2–4 tsp crushed aniseed and/or fennel
1 ¼ dl (½ cup) rye meal
about 4 dl (2 cups) wheat flour

Crumble the yeast into a bowl and stir in a little of the milk.

Melt the fat. Pour in the milk and heat gently until the mixture is lukewarm (37°C, 98°F).

Pour the milk over the yeast and stir in the salt, syrup, spices and about half the rye meal. Add the rest of the flour, alternating rye meal with wheat flour and finishing with the latter. Work the dough until it is smooth and viscous. Sprinkle a little flour on top, cover the dough with a cloth and leave to rise until it has doubled in size. Work the dough together in the mixing bowl; then lay it on a lightly floured pastry board and knead it until it is smooth.

Divide the dough into four. Roll each quarter into a ball, and then roll them out into cakes about 20 cm (8 inches) across. Press out a round hole in the centre of each cake. Put them on a greased baking tray to rise (about 30 minutes), prick them with a fork and bake them at 200°C (400°F) for 10–12 minutes.

Brush them with hot water when you remove them from the oven, and leave them to cool on a soft cloth, covered with another cloth.

FRESHLY BOILED POTATOES

NYKOKT VARM POTATIS

Steaming-hot, freshly boiled potatoes are a must on the smörgåsbord, since they alone permit the herring to be savored to the full. When new potatoes are in season, they should be boiled with dill. Preferably, they should be boiled in their jackets: cooked in this way, they taste better than if they are peeled when raw.

IN OUR SECOND trip round the smörgåsbord, we devote our attention to fish of various kinds: smoked, marinated, salted, poached and jellied.

Salmon is paramount among fish. This superb creature, with its delicate pink flesh, once formed part of the ordinary man's diet, at least in coastal settlements, but today is exorbitantly expensive. It is hard to believe that salmon was once so very common in Swedish waterways that maids and manservants in areas rich in salmon sometimes had an extra clause written into their contracts with local farming people, namely that salmon should not be set on the dinner table more than a specified number of times a week.

Salmon is found in many guises on the smörgåsbord – poached, marinated, smoked, chimney-smoked, salted and as pâté.

Scandinavian salmon *(Salmo salar)* are usually plump and good to eat, with tender yet firm flesh. The salmon caught in the Pacific (*Oncorhyncus*) is another subspecies – slimmer and with flesh which is redder, leaner and less tender. It is less suitable than Scandinavian salmon for smoking, marinating or salting. The color of the salmon comes from the food it eats. The eastern Atlantic salmon is not as red as the Pacific subspecies, but it is of much higher quality. It goes well with both smoked and marinated whitefish, and with other fish which are less exclusive in Sweden, such as bream, mackerel and Baltic herring. Smoked eel is a delicacy which many are overjoyed to come across. Eel – a speciality prized most, perhaps, in the southernmost regions of the country – is also served both poached and jellied, as well as in more specific ways, e.g. in Skåne it is salted, dried, smoked and then served hot with tartare sauce, or baked on rye straw ("luad" and "halmad" respectively).

Baltic herring reappears here in the form of several cold, oven-baked dishes made from the fresh, newly caught fish, and of "böckling", i.e. smoked.

Second-round dishes also include a bowl of crusty prawns, boiled in their shells. However, they almost require a round of their own, since the shelling process leaves so much behind on one's plate.

SECOND-ROUND DISHES

SMOKED FISH
POACHED SALMON, SALMON TROUT OR CHAR
POACHED SALMON FINS
DILL-CURED SALMON WITH FRIED SALMON SKIN AND
DILL-CURED SALMON SAUCE
FISH PÂTÉ
SALMON PÂTÉ WITH SMOKED SALMON
POACHED BALTIC HERRING
BALTIC HERRING IN TOMATO SAUCE
POACHED EEL
JELLIED EEL
EEL PÂTÉ
DILL-CURED SALMON SALAD
WEST COAST SALAD
TUNAFISH SALAD
SMOKED BALTIC HERRING SALAD
MARINATED SMOKED BALTIC HERRING
MARINATED MUSSELS
GARNISHED EGGS
PRAWNS
HORSERADISH CREAM
SHARP SAUCE
MAYONNAISE
RHODE ISLAND SAUCE
TABLE VINEGAR (1 PART WHITE SPIRIT VINEGAR, 12%,
2 PARTS WATER)

INKOKT LAX

approx. 2 kg (2 ½ lb) middle-cut
  salmon
a few dill stalks

FOR THE STOCK:
2 liters (5 ½ pints) water
½ dl (¼ cup) wine vinegar
2 tbsp salt
40 white peppercorns
1 piece of carrot in thin slices
1 small onion with 2 cloves stuck in it
¼ tsp thyme
1 bay leaf

Mix all the ingredients for the stock, bring to a boil and simmer for about 20 minutes.

Cut the salmon crosswise in 1 cm (¼ inch) slices. Put the slices into the simmering stock, which should just cover the fish. Pour away excess liquid.

Bring to the boil again, then remove immediately from the heat and leave the fish to cool in the stock, with the lid on.

Chill the fish thoroughly. Arrange the slices of salmon in a deep dish and pour a little of the stock on top. Garnish with some of the cooked onion and carrot slices, plus some fresh dill sprigs. Serve with mayonnaise, pickled gherkin and boiled potatoes with dill. Salmon trout and char can be cooked in the same way.

The head, gills, backbone, skin and fins of a freshly caught salmon (generously cut away, i.e. with some flesh remaining) may be boiled as in the above recipe for poached salmon, and left to cool. When they are thoroughly cooled, the pieces are placed in a bowl with a little stock and served with mayonnaise and pickled gherkins.

Salmon fins may also be jellied. Soften 2 teaspoons of gelatin in cold water. Take about 2 dl (¾ cup) of stock, heat it up and thoroughly mix in the gelatin. Pour the mixture over the boiled salmon fins in a bowl and chill until set, i.e. about 2 hours.

DILL-CURED SALMON WITH FRIED SALMON SKIN AND DILL-CURED SALMON SAUCE

GRAVAD LAX MED HALSTRADE LAXSKINN OCH GRAVLAXSÅS

"Gravning", also called "sockersaltning" ("sugar-salting") is a method of marinating fish specific to Sweden which makes the flesh tender and tasty after it has been left for a day or so. Generous amounts of white pepper and the typically Swedish herb dill also contribute to the delicious flavor.

All kinds of plump fish, such as whitefish, Baltic herring, salmon trout and mackerel, can be marinated in this way. The important thing is that the fish is absolutely fresh and has not been frozen.

For dill-cured salmon, take the following ingredients:

> approx. 1 kg (2 ½ lb) middle-cut salmon
> 1–2 tbsp oil
> 1 dl (½ cup) sugar
> 1 dl (½ cup) non-iodized salt
> 2 tsp crushed white peppercorns
> 2 dl (¾ cup) chopped dill

Wipe the salmon dry, but do not rinse it. Divide it in two along the backbone, and carefully remove all the bones – you can feel them if you stroke the surface with your fingertips, and they can easily be pulled out with pliers or strong tweezers. Coat the pieces of salmon with a little oil.

Mix the sugar, salt and white pepper, and rub this mixture on both sides of the salmon halves.

Sandwich the pieces of salmon together with dill, laying the fleshy sides together and the thin part against the thick. Put the salmon in a large plastic bag, surrounded by dill; close up the bag and put it in a dish. Place a cutting board or something similar on top, and a weight of some kind on it so as to keep the salmon under pressure.

Chill the salmon for at least 24–30 hours, preferably a couple of days. Turn the bag now and then during this time. Then scrape off the seasoning and discard the liquid which has accumulated in the dish.

Cut the salmon off the skin in thin, angled slices or 3 cm (1 inch) chunks. The skin is cut in 1 cm (¼ inch) strips, which are fried – skin side down – in a very hot dry pan until they are almost burned. Serve as a garnish to the cold salmon.

"Gravlaxsås" is served as an accompaniment to the dill-cured fish.

1 tbsp mild Swedish mustard
1 tsp dark French mustard
2 tsp sugar
1 ½ tbsp wine vinegar
salt, pepper
2 dl (¾ cup) oil (not olive oil)
chopped dill
(lemon juice)

Mix the mustard, sugar and vinegar and season with pinches of salt and pepper. Stir vigorously, mixing in the oil while you pour it in a steady stream. When the sauce has attained a mayonnaise-like consistency, stir in the chopped dill, together with a few drops of fresh lemon juice if desired.

FISH PÂTÉ

750 g (1 ½–2 lb) pike or pike perch
  with all bones carefully removed
3 egg whites
2 tsp salt
5 dl (2 ¼ cups) thick cream
¼ tsp white pepper
pinch of cayenne pepper
2 tbsp brandy
200 g (1 cup) shelled prawns
200 g (1 cup) boiled mussels
1 bunch of chives
1 bunch of dill
1 tbsp butter (for greasing dish)

Fillet the fish, remove all the bones, cut it in pieces and mix with the salt. Grind it as finely as possible (or use cutting blender). Chill it well, on ice or in the freezer.

Blend the fish with the egg whites, one at a time. Chill the mixture again.

Add the well-chilled cream gradually, stirring continuously, and season with white and cayenne pepper and brandy. Take a sample, fry it and check the seasoning. Chill the mixture again.

Blend the mixture with the prawns and mussels, cut in pieces, and the chopped herbs.

Pack the mixture into a well-buttered pâté mold. Smooth the surface and cover it with aluminum foil. Bake the pâté – with the dish standing in a pan of water or "bain marie" – for 40–50 minutes at 180°C (350°F). Be careful that the water in the bain marie does not boil. The temperature should not exceed 80–90°C (175–190°F). Test with a skewer to see if it is cooked right through. Allow it to cool, then chill it in the refrigerator.

To serve, unmold and cut in thin slices. It may also be served on its own, with Rhode Island sauce and boiled potatoes.

Salmon Pâté with Smoked Salmon

LAXPASTEJ MED RÖKT LAX

250 g (½ lb) skinned and boned
  salmon, diced
1 large, finely chopped shallot
3 eggs
6 dl (2 cups) thick cream
250 g (½ lb) frozen leaf spinach,
  thawed and coarsely chopped
1 egg
2 hard-boiled eggs
12 large, thin slices of smoked salmon
salt
cayenne pepper
nutmeg
butter

Make sure that the salmon is thoroughly chilled. Place it in the blender with the shallot, a little salt and cayenne pepper. Run the blender for 30 seconds. Then place the blender container in the refrigerator and leave it to stand for half an hour. Then turn on the blender again, add the eggs and then the cream, a little at a time. Replace in the refrigerator.

Squeeze as much liquid as possible out of the spinach and fry it for a little while in browned butter to remove more water. Season with salt, pepper and a little nutmeg. Turn the spinach out in a bowl and add an egg. Put it in the refrigerator.

Cut the hard-boiled eggs in large dice, together with two of the smoked salmon slices. These are then mixed with the spinach when it is thoroughly chilled.

Line an oblong mold with the smoked salmon slices so that they cover the whole bottom and sides. Let part of them hang over the edge so that the pâté may be wrapped up when the mold has been filled.

Take a few spoonfuls of the salmon mixture and mix it with the spinach. Spread half the salmon mixture in the mold. Hollow it out lengthwise.

Using a piping bag with a large nozzle, fill the furrow with spinach. Cover it with the rest of the salmon mixture. Smooth down the surface and fold the smoked salmon over it. Cover first with greased paper and then with aluminum foil.

Bake the pâté for one hour in a bain marie in a medium-hot oven (200°C, 400°F). The water should not be allowed to boil.

Leave the pâté to cool, and stand it in the refrigerator overnight. Cut it in thin slices, garnish with sprigs of dill and serve accompanied by dill mayonnaise.

POACHED BALTIC HERRING

INKOKT STRÖMMING

1 ½ kg (3-3 ½ lb) fresh
    Baltic herring
1 tsp salt
finely chopped dill

FOR THE STOCK:
2 dl (¾ cup) white spirit
    vinegar (12%)
5 dl (2 cups) water
1 bay leaf
10 white peppercorns
6 whole allspice
3 tsp sugar
1 ½ tsp salt

Clean the herring and remove the backbone. Rinse and dry the fish, and rub it with salt. Sprinkle a little finely chopped dill on the insides. In the meantime, bring the stock ingredients to a boil.

Roll up the herring fillets, with the skin on the outside, and lay them next to each other in a shallow saucepan. Pour the hot stock on top, bring to a boil and simmer for about 5 minutes. Leave to cool.

If so desired, the backbone may remain and the fish be cooked as follows. After cleaning, rinsing and salting the fish, lay them on a bed of dill, with the skins uppermost, in a saucepan. Pour on top a stock composed of water, salt, dill sprigs and stalks and simmer gently for 5–6 minutes. Leave the herring to cool in the stock, without a lid.

TOMATSTRÖMMING

500 g (1 lb) small Baltic herring
salt, white pepper
2 tbsp chopped dill

FOR THE SAUCE:
½ dl (¼ cup) oil
2 tbsp wine vinegar
3 tbsp tomato purée
1 tbsp finely chopped onion

Clean, rinse and bone the herring. Sprinkle with salt, pepper and chopped dill on the insides.

Mix the other ingredients to make a sauce. Spread a thin layer of sauce in the bottom of an ovenproof dish. Roll the herring – with the skins on the outside – into tight bundles and pack them together in the dish; distribute the rest of the sauce evenly on top. The dish should be just large enough to accommodate the herring rolls.

Sprinkle a little oil over the dish and put it in a hot oven (approx. 200°C, 400°F), under a tight-fitting lid, to braise for 20–30 minutes. Leave to cool, without removing the lid.

As a hot dish in its own right, Baltic herring in tomato sauce is served with boiled potatoes.

INKOKT ÅL

1 eel
5 dl (2–2 ½ cups) water
½ tbsp salt
2 tbsp white spirit vinegar (12%)
6 white peppercorns
dill

Skin the eel, rinse it and cut it into pieces. These should be less than 2 cm (an inch) wide where the diameter of the eel is greatest, and increase in width as the eel gets thinner.

Mix the water, salt and spirit vinegar in a saucepan and bring to a boil. Add the eel. Skim, mix in the dill and white pepper and leave to simmer for 20 minutes.

Transfer the eel to another pan and strain the stock on top. Chill. Serve the poached eel thoroughly chilled, with table vinegar as a condiment on the smörgåsbord. (Table vinegar is a blend of one part white spirit (12%) vinegar and two parts water.)

Poached eel is an excellent supper dish, accompanied by boiled potatoes, fresh green salad and sharp sauce (see p. 61).

JELLIED EEL

ÅLALADÅB

1 large or 2 small eels
salt, white pepper
1 dl (½ cup) chopped dill
1 liter (2 pints) water
2 tbsp white spirit
   vinegar (12%)
2 tsp salt
10 white peppercorns

1 bunch of dill sprigs
green part of one leek
1 small carrot

FOR THE JELLY:
¾ dl (¼ cup) stock
2 egg whites
8 tsp gelatin

Skin, clean and rinse the eel well under the faucet. If the eel is newly caught, put it in a bucket with a handful of salt strewn on top, and the lid on to prevent it leaping out.

Slit the eel open and remove all bones. Sprinkle salt, pepper and chopped dill on the inside of the split eel, and then roll it up tightly and fasten the bundle with twine.

Mix the water, spirit vinegar, salt, white peppercorns, some stalks of dill, the leek and carrot (sliced) and bring to a boil. Add the eel roll and simmer gently for 30 minutes. Leave the eel to cool in the stock.

To make the jelly, mix ¾ dl (¼ cup) of the cold stock with the egg whites and the gelatin, which should already have been soaked in water. Bring slowly to a boil, stirring constantly. Simmer for a while, then strain the stock. Leave to cool, but do not allow it to set. Cut the rolled-up eel crosswise in thin slices.

Chill a jellied eel mold thoroughly, by placing it in the freezer for some time, or in a bowl of iced water. Pour in a few spoonfuls of the cold (but not set) jelly, and rotate the mold until it is lined with a layer of set jelly throughout.

Now distribute slices of eel evenly around the inside of the mold, here and there decorating with sprigs of dill. Pour in more jelly, and fill with the rest of the eel, followed by the remaining jelly. Chill the mold thoroughly.

Unmold the jellied eel. It comes away easily if you dip the mold momentarily in hot water. Garnish with dill.

If it is to be served on its own as a dinner dish, jellied eel should be accompanied by mayonnaise, sharp sauce (see p. 61) or horseradish cream (see p. 60) and boiled potatoes.

ÅLPASTEJ

500 g (1 lb) pike fillet, with all the
　　bones carefully removed
200 g (6 oz) eel fillets, about
　　8 inches long
½ dl (¼ cup) white wine
2–3 tsp salt
½ tsp white pepper
1 tbsp chopped chives
2 tbsp chopped parsley
1 tsp tarragon
1 tbsp chopped fresh chervil
a few finely chopped mushrooms
1 large egg white
2 tsp brandy
generous pinch cayenne pepper
5 dl (2 ¼ cups) thick cream
1 dl (½ cup) breadcrumbs (made
　　from one-day-old white bread)

Marinate the eel fillets in the white wine mixed with ½–1 tsp salt, pepper, chives, half the parsley and tarragon, chervil and mushrooms for about 2 hours.

Then simmer the eel fillets for 10 minutes in the marinade. Leave to cool, then chill thoroughly.

Grind the pike fillets very finely (or put them in the blender). Mix the egg white, salt and brandy with the pike; add the cayenne pepper and then, gradually, the cream. Chill the mixture.

Mix the breadcrumbs with the rest of the parsley and tarragon. Add 1 tbsp of eel marinade, and blend well.

Put half the pike mixture in a greased, oblong dish, and top with the breadcrumb mixture. Place the eel fillets (well drained) on top, and then top with the rest of the pike mixture. Cover with foil and bake in a bain marie at 175°C (340°F) for about 40 minutes. Be careful that the water in the bain marie does not boil. The temperature should not exceed 80–90°C (175–190°F).

DILL-CURED SALMON SALAD

GRAVLAXSALLAD

400 g (1 lb) dill-cured salmon, cubed
4 hard-boiled eggs
shredded lettuce leaves
asparagus
dill crowns
a little dill-cured salmon sauce (see p. 46)

Cut the hard-boiled eggs in two; dice four halves and slice the other four in thin wedges. Mix the cubes of dill-cured salmon with the diced egg and "gravlax" sauce. Put the mixture on a bed of shredded lettuce. Garnish with the egg wedges, some sticks of asparagus and dill crowns.

This is a good way of using up leftover dill-cured salmon.

WEST COAST SALAD

VÄSTKUSTSALLAD

boiled lobster, cut in small pieces
shelled prawns
boiled mussels, well drained
fresh mushrooms, sliced
peeled tomatoes with seeds removed,
    cut in wedges
lettuce
green peas
(quantities may be varied according
    to one's means)

FOR THE DRESSING:
1 dl (½ cup) oil
½ dl (¼ cup) white wine vinegar
salt, freshly ground white pepper
1 tsp dark French mustard
2 tsp finely chopped dill

Mix all the ingredients for the salad. Shake the dressing ingredients together and pour it over the salad. Chill.

Serve on a bed of finely shredded lettuce.

Tunafish Salad

TONFISKSALLAD

1 can tunafish (approx. 200 g, 6 oz)
1 small lettuce
4 tomatoes
1 leek
a few sticks of celery
cold cooked French beans
1 dl (½ cup) green peas
10–12 olives
1 clove of garlic

FOR THE VINAIGRETTE DRESSING:
1 tbsp wine vinegar
2 tbsp oil
salt, pepper, paprika and thyme to taste

Rub the salad bowl with the clove of garlic. Shred the lettuce, cut the tomatoes in small wedges and the leek and celery in pieces and place them on top of the lettuce. Distribute the French beans, peas and olives on top. Divide the tunafish into smallish pieces and lay it in a pile in the middle.

Mix the ingredients for the vinaigrette dressing and pour it over the salad.

Small pieces of cleaned, filleted smoked Baltic herring are served in a vinaigrette dressing (with a little mustard, if desired, to taste) with one of the following sets of accompaniments:

1. diced apples and boiled potatoes, chopped onion;
2. boiled potatoes and pickled beets, diced;
3. prawns, tomato wedges, diced apple and sliced radishes.

The ingredients are piled up on a dish with the smoked herring and the vinaigrette dressing is poured on top.

Another alternative is to mix pieces of smoked herring with diced apples, potatoes and pickled beets. Take care when mixing the salad ingredients, so that the salad does not begin to look pulpy. Mix finely chopped herbs in the vinaigrette dressing and pour it over the salad.

Marinated Smoked Baltic Herring

MARINERAD BÖCKLING

Skin several smoked herrings; clean and bone them thoroughly. Arrange them on a serving dish, and pour on top a dressing made of one part wine vinegar to two parts oil blended with a little unsweetened mustard, salt, pepper, finely chopped onion, finely chopped capers and chopped parsley.

Marinated Mussels

MARINERADE MUSSLOR

This dish is not to be confused with moules marinières.

Brush the mussels clean under the faucet, then place them in a saucepan with a little finely chopped onion, black pepper, 1 tbsp oil and a little white wine (or the juice of half a lemon). Bring to a boil under a tight-fitting lid, and leave to cool without removing the lid. Break off one of the shell halves of each mussel, laying them in a dish as you do so, with each mussel in the remaining half-shell. Reduce the stock until very little remains; when it is cool, mix it with mayonnaise and a little thick cream. Add salt, pepper and lemon juice to taste. Cover each mussel with a dab of sauce, and strew chopped parsley or dill on top.

SWEDISH CAVIAR EGGS

KAVIARÄGG

Place 1 tsp caviar cream (whipped cream mixed with a little salted Swedish caviar from a can) on half a hard-boiled egg. Garnish with a dill crown.

BLEAK ROE EGGS

LÖJROMSÄGG

Put 1 tsp bleak roe and a thin slice of onion on half a hard-boiled egg.

PRAWN EGGS

RÄKÄGG

Put a teaspoonful of mayonnaise on half a hard-boiled egg and lay a shelled prawn on top. Put the egg halves on a bed of shredded lettuce, and garnish with lemon wedges.

EGGS VINAIGRETTE

ÄGG VINÄGRETT

4 hard-boiled eggs
4 bowl-shaped lettuce leaves
4 Swedish anchovy fillets

FOR THE DRESSING:
3 tbsp oil
1 tbsp white wine vinegar
2 tbsp finely chopped dill
a little salt and white pepper

Carefully remove the yolks from the hard-boiled eggs. Make the dressing; chop the whites and mix them in.

Divide the mixture between the four lettuce leaves arranged on a serving dish. Lay the yolks on top, and curl an anchovy fillet around each.

EGGS VINAIGRETTE WITH ASPARAGUS

ÄGG VINÄGRETT MED SPARRIS

Replace the dill in the preceding recipe by chopped parsley. Chop up the entire egg and mix in the dressing. Place boiled asparagus on a bed of thinly sliced tomatoes and spread the mixture on top.

EGGS VINAIGRETTE WITH SMOKED BALTIC HERRING

ÄGG VINÄGRETT MED BÖCKLING

Place the smoked Baltic herring fillets on a bed of thinly sliced onion and pour egg dressing (see preceding recipe) on top.

MUSTARD EGGS

SENAPSÄGG

4 cold hard-boiled eggs
shredded lettuce
3 tbsp crabmeat
2–3 tbsp chopped chives

FOR THE DRESSING:
2 ½ dl (1 cup) sour cream
2 tsp French mustard
salt, white pepper

Cut the hard-boiled eggs in two crosswise. Put the halves on a bed of shredded lettuce. Mix the dressing and pour it over the eggs. Garnish with alternate bands of crabmeat and chives.

Curry Eggs

CURRYÄGG

Place the hard-boiled eggs – cut in half lengthwise – in a circle on a serving dish. Garnish each egg with a dab of curry mayonnaise and half a green olive. Mix a dressing of mayonnaise and thick, unwhipped cream. Flavor it strongly with curry powder. Pour the dressing into the middle of the circle and pile up cold, boiled, shelled prawns generously in the center.

Prawns

RÄKOR

Unshelled prawns are an intrinsic part of the smörgåsbord. They are served cold, but not on ice since this inhibits their fine aroma. A fingerbowl with a slice of lemon in it is a necessity for each guest, since one has to use one's hands as implements when eating prawns in their natural state.

Horseradish Cream

PEPPARROTSGRÄDDE

1 ½ dl (½ cup) whipping cream
½ tsp sugar
½ tsp white spirit vinegar (12%)
2 tbsp grated horseradish

Whip the cream until stiff. Add the sugar, vinegar and horseradish. Good with cold poached fish.

1 raw egg yolk
1 hard-boiled egg yolk
2 tsp mustard powder
3 tsp wine vinegar
2 dl (¾ cup) oil (preferably olive oil)
2 dl (¾ cup) whipping cream
1 tbsp very finely chopped dill

Tip the raw egg yolk into a basin. Sieve the hard-boiled yolk into the basin; add the mustard powder and vinegar followed by the oil, initially one drop at a time and then in a thin stream, whisking vigorously all the while. Lightly whip the cream and stir it in. Finally, add the finely chopped dill.

Mayonnaise

MAJONNÄS

2 egg yolks
3 tsp wine vinegar
2 tsp French mustard
3–4 dl (1 ½ cups) oil
salt, cayenne pepper

Mix all the ingredients except for the oil. They – and the mixing bowl – should be at room temperature. Pour the oil into a jug so that you can then easily pour it (at first, a drop at a time) steadily in, while stirring rhythmically and constantly. Should the mayonnaise by some misfortune curdle, all is not lost: take a new bowl, another egg yolk and a pinch of mustard and begin again, stirring vigorously and carefully while gradually pouring in the curdled mayonnaise.

Dill Mayonnaise

DILLMAJONNÄS

Blend a generous quantity of finely chopped dill into the mayonnaise.

Rhode Island Sauce

RHODE ISLAND-SÅS

Flavor the mayonnaise with chili sauce and finely chopped fresh red pepper. If desired, whipped cream may be added to give the sauce a lighter consistency.

WE HAVE NOW reached the meat stage of the smörgåsbord, at which cold cuts of various kinds are set out on the table. For example, there is thinly sliced smoked reindeer meat: the care of reindeer is still an important means of livelihood for the people of Sweden's northernmost region, Lapland. There is sauna-smoked ham, a tender variant of smoked ham; leg of mutton, salted, dried and thinly sliced; all sorts of roast joints, similarly cut in thin slices and accompanied by suitable side dishes such as green salad, potato salad, pickled gherkins, salted gherkins, gherkins in spirit vinegar and cucumber preserve, as well as tomato preserve and various sorts of mustard. Potted meats, sausages and jellied meats also belong to this round, particularly on the Christmas table.

Swedish liver pâté – flavored with Swedish anchovies! – is another must, as is jellied veal for those who want a low-fat, mild and nutritious meal; and then of course there should be several salads.

Let the food itself adorn the dish, and never garnish with items which do not naturally belong with it. Thus shavings of horseradish on the roast beef are good, but canned mandarin segments on the meat are an abomination.

THIRD-ROUND DISHES

ASSORTED COLD CUTS
DRIED LEG OF MUTTON
GERMAN AND OTHER SAUSAGES
YULE HAM
BOILED PIG'S TROTTERS
BOILED, SMOKED PIG'S HEAD
PORK IN ASPIC
JELLIED VEAL
PORK BRAWN
COLLARED BRAWN
PRUNE-STUFFED SPARE RIBS
ROAST SALTED SPARE RIBS
SALT LEG OF BEEF
SWEDISH LIVER PÂTÉ
CHICKEN SALAD
SAUSAGE SALAD
CHEESE SALAD
POTATO SALAD
SCANDINAVIAN SALAD
EGG SALAD
PICKLED BEETS
OLD-FASHIONED PICKLED CUCUMBER
RED CABBAGE SALAD
GREEN TOMATO PRESERVE
ASSORTED VARIETIES OF MUSTARD
BOWL OF FRESH GREEN SALAD

DRIED LEG OF MUTTON

FÅRFIOL

"Fårfiol" is the name for a salted, dried and sometimes also smoked leg of mutton. It is an allusion to the shape of the meat: "får" means sheep, while "fiol" means violin. It is served cold, cut in thin slices, on the smörgåsbord, and with scrambled eggs or creamed potatoes as a dish in its own right.

YULE HAM

JULSKINKA

Mustard-glazed Yule ham is the most important component of the Swedish Christmas table. Nowadays, it is bought ready for boiling or baking, i.e. it is lightly "sugar-salted" – cured – and sometimes also slightly smoked. These days, many people choose to buy boned ham. After boiling, it is grilled after brushing with a mixture of mustard and egg. The ham stock – after removal of fat – is used for another traditional Christmas dish, bread dipped in ham broth (see p. 126).

> 1 lightly salted, perhaps slightly
>   smoked ham weighing 3–5 kg
>   (6–11 lb)
> the green part of a leek
> some parsley stalks
> 1 bay leaf
> 1 sprig of fresh thyme or ¼ tsp
>   dried thyme
>
> FOR THE GLAZE:
> 4–5 tbsp sweet Swedish mustard
> 1 tbsp mustard powder
> 1 tbsp syrup
> 2 egg yolks
> 1 tbsp potato flour
> 1 dl (½ cup) breadcrumbs

Rinse the ham, put it in a large saucepan and pour in enough water to cover it. Bring rapidly to a boil and boil for several minutes. Discard the water, and fill anew; bring to a boil again, and skim if necessary. Add the vegetables and seasoning, preferably tied together with string. Stick an oven thermometer into the thickest part of the ham (not against the bone), and let the ham gradually become more tender as it simmers, over a low heat and with a tight-fitting lid on top, until the temperature shows approx. 70°C (160°F) (if the ham is smoked 65°C, 150°F). Leave the ham to cool in its broth, as rapidly as possible.

Trim the skin from the ham and put it on a roasting rack over a baking pan.

Mix all the ingredients for the glaze, except for the breadcrumbs. Spread the mixture over the ham, and then scatter the breadcrumbs on top. Sprinkle with a little melted butter. Bake in a hot oven (about 200–225°C, 420°F) until the glaze is an attractive golden color. Keep the broth from the ham for "Dip in the Pot" (see p. 126).

BOILED PIG'S TROTTERS

KOKTA GRISFÖTTER

6 pig's feet
6 tbsp salt
¼ tsp soda

FOR THE BRINE:
2 liters (4 pints) water
2 tbsp sugar
1 dl (½ cup) non-iodized sea salt

Soak the pig's feet in cold water to cover for 24 hours or so, changing the water from time to time. Scald them in boiling water and scrape them thoroughly.

Place the feet in a large saucepan in cold, slightly salt water to which the soda has been added. The best results are obtained by cooking the trotters whole, so that they do not lose their shape. Simmer gently, under cover, for about 3 ½ hours; test with a skewer to see if they are ready.

Remove the feet, rinse them under the faucet and put them in a bowl or casserole. Meanwhile, make a brine of water, sugar and coarse, non-iodized salt. Bring to the boil and skim; leave it to cool. Finally, pour it over the trotters.

For the smörgåsbord it is advisable to cut the cooked and rinsed trotters in pieces.

White spirit vinegar and pickled beets should be served as accompaniments.

Boiled, Smoked Pig's Head

KOKT RÖKT GRISHUVUD

Take a slightly salted, and lightly smoked, pig's head and soak it in cold water for at least 12 hours, in a large saucepan. Take it out, scrape and wipe it thoroughly. Tie it up in a large linen cloth and return it to the saucepan, with sufficient fresh, cold water just to cover it; bring to a boil. Skim well, and leave it to simmer under cover on a very low heat until tender (about 2 ½ hours).

Remove the bundle, untie the cloth and leave the head to drain and cool. It should be given pride of place on the smörgåsbord and decorated with curly kale, a red apple in the mouth and parsley in the ears.

Pork in Aspic

FLÄSKALADÅB

1 kg (2 lb) fresh, lean shoulder
　of pork on the bone
½ kg (1 lb) veal shank bone
(1 calf's foot)
1–2 tbsp salt
1 ½ liters (3 pints) water
1 carrot
2–3 whole cloves
1 bay leaf
5–6 whole white peppercorns
2–3 whole allspice

For the aspic:
1 liter (2 pints) skimmed or strained stock
3–4 tsp gelatin
1–2 whisked egg whites
1 ½ tbsp white spirit vinegar (12%)

For the garnish:
2 hard-boiled eggs, cut in wedges
2 pickled beets, sliced
small sprigs of parsley

Ask your butcher to halve the veal shank and calf's foot lengthwise. Rinse the veal and pork, rub in half the salt and place them together in a saucepan. Add cold water to cover. Bring to a boil and boil vigorously for several minutes. Skim thoroughly. Add more salt if necessary, together with the peeled carrot and the other seasoning. Simmer gently, with the pan covered, until the meat is tender and comes away from the bone easily – about 2 hours.

Remove the pork and leave to cool. Leave the veal shank simmering with the seasoning in the stock until about one liter (two pints) of liquid remain. Strain the stock, leave it to cool and skim off all the fat. Then mix the ingredients for the aspic and bring them to a boil, whisking continuously. Do not use gelatin if you have used a calf's foot in the making of the stock.

Remove the pan from the heat, cover and leave the mixture to stand for 8–10 minutes. Then strain through a cloth dipped in hot water and wrung out. Allow the jelly to cool, but not to set.

Cut the pork in small, even dice and prepare the eggs, beets and parsley for the garnish. Rinse a mold with cold water, pour a little jelly into the bottom and leave it to set. Garnish attractively but sparingly with the egg wedges, beet slices and small parsley sprigs. Taking the utmost care, pour in a little more jelly, to set and thereby hold the garnish in position. Now fill the mold with the pork dice and stick a few parsley sprigs and beet slices down the sides here and there. Pour on the rest of the jelly, carefully stir the dice so that they move freely in the jelly, and then chill the mold in the refrigerator, preferably overnight.

Dip the mold in hot water for a moment, dry it rapidly with kitchen paper and carefully tip the jellied pork out on the serving dish. Serve with, for example, sharp sauce (see p. 61) or curry mayonnaise, pickled beets and freshly boiled dill potatoes.

These quantities on the smörgåsbord should be enough for 8–10 people. Table vinegar should always be at hand when jellied dishes of this kind are served.

1 kg (2 lb) veal shank with bone
1 kg (2 lb) neck of veal, with bone
½ tbsp crushed white peppercorns
ham broth
1 onion, sliced
1 carrot, sliced
bouquet garni consisting of 1 sprig of thyme,
   10 allspice, 1 bay leaf, 3 cloves

Rinse the meat well, break the bones and put them together in a saucepan. Pour on ham broth or water to cover the meat. Bring to a boil and skim well before adding the white peppercorns, vegetables and bouquet garni. Simmer until the meat is tender and easily comes away from the bone. Remove the meat and dice it finely.

Strain the stock thoroughly through a linen cloth so that it is smooth and clear. Pour about 1 ½ liters (3 pints) of the stock into a saucepan and add the diced meat. Season well, perhaps adding a little salt. Bring to the boil and then pour the mixture into molds, which should then be chilled so that the jelly sets.

When the jelly is cold but still not set, give the mixture in the mold a stir.

If the jelly has still not set by the following day, put it back in a pan and warm it enough for some teaspoons of gelatin softened in cold water to be dissolved in the mixture. Stir it in well. Pour the mixture back in the mold and chill once more.

Jellied veal should not be too hard in consistency.

PRESSYLTA

In olden times, pork brawn was made from a pig's head. But very few people have access to the genuine article nowadays! Here is a recipe for a much less greasy form of brawn, the preparation of which is a great deal simpler than that of headcheese or pig's head brawn.

1 kg (2 lb) shoulder of pork
500 g (1 lb) shoulder of veal
2 good-sized pieces of pork rind
3 tbsp salt
1 carrot
1 large onion
4 cloves
8 white peppercorns
1 bay leaf
300 g (1 ¼ cups) pork fat, thinly sliced

FOR THE SEASONING:
2 tsp crushed allspice
1 ½ tsp ginger
1 tbsp salt

Place the pork, veal and rind in a large casserole and fill with water so that the meat is barely covered. Bring the water to a boil. Skim. Add salt, sliced carrot, the onion larded with cloves, peppercorns and bay leaf. Simmer the meat very gently until it is tender. Separate the fat and lean meat. Leave to cool, and then cut all the meat in thin slices. Strain the stock. Wash the casserole and pour the stock back.

Wring out a cloth in hot water and line a bowl with it.

Cut the fat from the pieces of rind, and line the bowl with thin slices of fat and strips of rind, letting the fat protrude somewhat at the edges. Grind the remaining rind – it makes an excellent binding agent.

Mix the seasoning. Place the meat and fat in alternating layers in the bowl, sprinkling a little seasoning mixture between layers. Spread a little of the ground rind on each layer too; this is particularly important if the meat is lean.

Press the mixture together by hand, fold the lard over on top and bring the edges of the cloth together, tying them as tightly as possible with string.

Lower the brawn into the stock, bring to a boil and then simmer gently for 35–40 minutes. Remove the brawn, lay it on a flat dish and put a plate on top. Place a weight of some kind on the plate, and leave the brawn in a cool place, weighted down. Chill overnight before removing the cloth. The stock is excellent when used for "Dip in the Pot" (see p. 126).

The pork brawn may be kept for some time in salty brine.

COLLARED BRAWN

RULLSYLTA

1 ½ kg (3 lb) flank of veal or mutton
1 + 1 tbsp salt
½ tbsp sugar
1 tsp saltpeter
1 tsp crushed white pepper
2 tsp crushed allspice
½ tsp crushed juniper berries
2 thin slices of pork fat

FOR THE STOCK:
veal or mutton bones
1 small carrot
1 small onion
1 bay leaf
some white peppercorns
several sprigs of parsley

Remove all bone and cartilage from the meat. Tear off the outermost dry membrane of the mutton. Mix the salt, sugar and saltpeter and rub the mixture into the meat.

Spread out the meat well and distribute the crushed peppercorns, juniper berries, 1 tbsp salt and the slices of fat on top. Roll up the meat as tightly as possible and tie up the roll securely with cotton thread. Chill for a day or so.

Make a white stock by boiling the bones with the carrot, onion, bay leaf, pepper and sprigs of parsley.

Place the roll in the stock and simmer until it is tender, i.e. about one hour. Leave it to cool, compressed by a weight. Serve cold on the smörgåsbord. The stock is excellent for "Dip in the Pot" (see p. 126).

PRUNE-STUFFED SPARE RIBS

PLOMMONSPÄCKAT REVBENSSPJÄLL

1 kg (2 lb) fresh spare ribs
pitted prunes
salt, white pepper
1 tsp ginger
½ tsp sage

Select a lean, but not too thin, section of spare ribs. Crack the bones, wipe and scrape the meat thoroughly. With a long, narrow knife, make deep slits in the sides of the meat and press in the prunes. Sprinkle the salt and pepper on top, and rub in the other seasoning.

Place the spare ribs with the fat side uppermost on an oven rack over a baking pan. Pour 1–2 dl water (about half a cup) onto the pan under the rack and roast the spare ribs in a medium-hot oven (approx. 200°C, 400°F) for 1 ½–2 hours, until the meat comes away easily from the bone. Baste frequently with the juices from the roasting pan, adding more water if the pan seems to be getting too dry.

Serve the spare ribs either hot or cold, on the Christmas table or the large smörgåsbord.

As a main dish, spare ribs are served hot with red cabbage and boiled or puréed potatoes. The prunes are placed in a bowl beside the meat.

ROAST SALTED SPARE RIBS

STEKT RIMMAT REVBENSSPJÄLL

Crack the bones and wipe the spare ribs carefully. Rub them with white pepper and ginger. Roast in the oven in the same way as for the prune-stuffed spare ribs in the previous recipe. Serve them cold and in slices on the smörgåsbord, or hot with red cabbage and fairly sour apple purée as a main dish.

SALTRULLE

The silverside (the hind leg muscle of the ox) is one of the toughest cuts of beef. But when salted and well boiled it tastes excellent. It may be served hot with puréed potatoes or cold, in thin slices, on the smörgåsbord.

The same recipe may also be used for ox tongue.

> 1 salted silverside of beef
> water
> 1 carrot
> 1 onion
> 1 bay leaf
> 5 whole allspice
> several sprigs of parsley

Put the meat in a saucepan, and pour in water to cover. Bring to a boil and skim well. Add the peeled carrot and onion, seasoning and parsley. Simmer on a low heat, with the lid on, until the meat is tender – about 2 hours. Test with a skewer: it should slide easily through the meat.

Leave to cool in the broth. Cut in thin slices.

If you do not have access to a ready-salted silverside of beef, perform the salting process as follows: rub the meat, after tying it up firmly, with a mixture of 5 tbsp salt, 2 tbsp sugar and 1 tsp saltpeter. Let the meat stand in the liquid which accumulates, keeping it in the refrigerator for 2–3 days and turning it morning and evening. Rinse and cook as above.

SVENSK LEVERPASTEJ

500 g (1 lb) calf's or pig's
   liver (or 250 g, ½ lb, of each)
milk
½ finely chopped onion
250 g (½ lb) pork fat, and a few
   large, thin slices of fat for the mold
3 cleaned, skinned and boned
   Swedish anchovy fillets
4 eggs
2 tbsp plain flour
1 tbsp potato flour
3 dl (1 ¼ cups) thick cream
1–2 tsp salt
white pepper
(quatre épices)
2 tbsp brandy or madeira

Soak the liver in milk overnight. Remove it, wipe it dry and cut it into large pieces. Sauté, but do not brown, the onion. Grind the pork fat two or three times, using the finest disc of the grinder (or use the blender), and then grind the liver, fat, onion and anchovies three times.

Whisk together the eggs, flour and cream and work the mixture, a little at a time, into the liver. Season with salt, pepper, a little quatre épices and brandy or madeira. Fry a little to check the seasoning. The pâté should have a fairly strong flavor.

Line the bottom and sides of a pâté mold, oblong bread pan or other ovenproof dish with thin slices of pork fat. Tip the mixture into the mold, but without filling it to the brim. Cover the surface with a pricked piece of greaseproof paper, cut to size and well greased; then cover the mold with aluminum foil and bake the pâté in a bain marie in a hot (200°C, 400°F) oven for 1–1 ½ hours. Test with a skewer to make sure the pâté is cooked right through.

Leave to cool. It may be garnished with aspic, if desired.

CHICKEN SALAD

Leftover boiled or roast chicken is diced and mixed with slices of raw mushrooms; celery, finely sliced crosswise; diced cooking apple and a few coarsely crushed walnuts. Bind with a little mayonnaise.

SAUSAGE SALAD

4 cold, boiled frankfurter
    sausages (or equivalent quantity of
    smoked German sausage)
4 cold boiled potatoes, preferably
    boiled in their jackets and then peeled
1 small pickled gherkin, or 1 piece
    of salted cucumber, cut into small pieces
1 tbsp capers
1 tbsp finely chopped chives
1 tbsp grated horseradish
1 tbsp chopped parsley

FOR THE DRESSING:
1 tsp dark French mustard
1 tsp Swedish mustard
1 tbsp wine vinegar
3 tbsp oil
½ clove of garlic, crushed
salt, white pepper

Cut the sausage and potato in small slices. Whisk the dressing ingredients together and season well with salt and pepper. Blend all the ingredients thoroughly with the dressing. Cover the salad and put it to one side for a few hours before serving. A few chopped fresh herbs on top do not go amiss.

CHEESE SALAD

OSTSALLAD

Coarsely shred some Swiss-type cheese and mix it with finely chopped celery and mayonnaise.

POTATO SALAD

POTATISSALLAD

Thinly slice some boiled potatoes and mix with a little finely chopped onion, finely chopped pickled beets and capers. Pour vinaigrette sauce on top.

SCANDINAVIAN SALAD

SKANDINAVISK SALLAD

> 75 g (½ cup) boiled tongue, shredded
> 75 g (½ cup) boiled ham, shredded
> 75 g (½ cup) veal, shredded
> 1 apple, shredded
> ½ salted cucumber, cut in sticks
> 150 g (1 cup) mayonnaise
> 4 lettuce leaves
> 1 hard-boiled egg cut in 4 wedges
> 1 tomato cut in 4 wedges
> 1 sprig of parsley

Mix the tongue, ham, veal, apple and salted cucumber. Stir in the mayonnaise and lay the salad on a bed of lettuce leaves. Garnish with egg, tomato and parsley.

Egg Salad

ÄGGSALLAD

Arrange hard-boiled egg wedges on lettuce leaves and cover with a light mayonnaise rather strongly flavored with dark French mustard.

Pickled Beets

INLAGDA RÖDBETOR

1 kg (2 lb) fresh beets

FOR THE PICKLE:
1 ½ dl (½ cup) white
    spirit vinegar (12%)
5 dl (2 cups) water
1 ½ dl (½ cup) sugar
6–7 cloves

Scrub the beets clean, leaving the root tips intact; simmer them in water. This takes considerably longer in winter than in summer, when they are young and fresh. Rinse them in cold water and then peel them.

Bring to a boil the spirit vinegar, water, sugar and cloves. Put the cold beets in the pickle, and leave them to stand for a day or so before serving.

If the beets are to be kept for a longish period, they should be boiled for a while in the pickle. A piece of horseradish in the pickle enables the beets to keep longer.

OLD-FASHIONED PICKLED CUCUMBER

GAMMALDAGS PRESSGURKA

Pickled cucumber is a good old traditional accompaniment of everyday Swedish fare. A few decades ago, roast veal with cream sauce, boiled potatoes and pickled cucumber was the classic Swedish Sunday dinner. Pickled cucumber gives a fresh flavor contrast with all kinds of boiled and roast meat, as well as with poached salmon.

    1 medium-sized cucumber
    a little salt
    1 dl (½ cup) white spirit vinegar (12%)
    1 dl (½ cup) water
    ½ dl (¼ cup) sugar
    ¼ tsp freshly ground white pepper
    2 tbsp finely chopped parsley

Peel the cucumber and slice it thinly. Put the slices into a bowl, salting slightly between layers. Place a similar bowl on top and weight it down. Leave to stand for about one hour.

Mix a dressing of spirit vinegar, water, sugar, white pepper and parsley. Stir until the sugar is dissolved.

Discard the liquid which has collected around the pressed cucumber. Pour the dressing over the slices of cucumber and chill the salad for several hours before serving.

RED CABBAGE SALAD

RÖDKÅLSSALLAD

    ¼ red cabbage, thinly sliced
    juice of one lemon
    1 dl (½ cup) water
    1 tbsp honey
    1 tsp salt

Mix the lemon juice, water, salt and honey, and bring the red cabbage to the boil in this mixture. Simmer, with the lid on, for about 1 hour.

Serve the cabbage either hot or cold with various kinds of meat.

GREEN TOMATO PRESERVE

1 kg (2 lb) small, uniformly
   green tomatoes

FOR THE PICKLE:
2 dl (¾ cup) white spirit vinegar (12%)
3 dl (1 ¼ cups) water
4–5 dl (2 cups) sugar
½ tsp whole cloves
2 small sticks of cinnamon
2 sticks of ginger

Trim, rinse, dry and prick the tomatoes. Simmer them in lightly salted water for 10–15 minutes, or until they are fairly soft.

Bring to the boil a pickle of spirit vinegar, water, sugar and spices. Skim, add the tomatoes and let them simmer gently until they are very soft. Remove them and put them in jars.

Bring the pickle to the boil again, strain off the spices and pour it over the tomatoes. Leave them to cool and replace the lids on the jars, or cover with muslin held in place by rubber bands.

This section of the smörgåsbord is called "småvarmt" (the hot buffet): the name alone evokes fine-flavored goodness. Gathered here are a number of hot dishes based on both fish and meat. Salt herring and fresh Baltic herring return in new guises, cooked in the oven or on top of the stove and served hot. These fourth-round dishes comprise a selection of light, tasty items which are in keeping with the basic idea of the smörgåsbord's completeness and wide range of variations.

The hot buffet should ideally include one salty dish, one very mild and easily digestible and one that is somewhat more solid. A common and appropriate combination is Jansson's temptation, meatballs and ovenbaked omelet plus, for example, creamed sweetbreads. There are numerous possible variations. The hot buffet also provides splendid opportunities for using up small leftovers of one kind and another.

In order to approach the smörgåsbord in a thoroughly systematic way and not to leave anything out, one should perhaps partake of the salty fourth-round dishes as a course in themselves, between the first and second rounds, forming the basis for the "little half" (the second glass of snaps).

JANSSON'S TEMPTATION
FRIED SWEDISH ANCHOVIES OR SMOKED BALTIC
HERRING
SMOKED BALTIC HERRING CASSEROLE
BALTIC HERRING WITH SWEDISH CAVIAR
HERRING PATTIES WITH CURRANT SAUCE
HERRING AU GRATIN
HERRING AU GRATIN WITH DILL
SALMON PUDDING
HERRING PUDDING WITH POTATOES
FRIED SALMON FINS
FRIED BALTIC HERRING FILLETS
FRIED BALTIC HERRING, OPERAKÄLLAREN STYLE
CHIMNEY SWEEPS
FRESH EEL ROASTED ON RYE STRAW
SALT SMOKED EEL
SALTED EEL
BOILED SALTED EEL
GRILLED SALTED EEL
CHRISTMAS SAUSAGE
VÄRMLAND SAUSAGE
FRIED PIG'S TROTTERS
BOILED LAMB IN DILL SAUCE
SWEDISH BEEFBURGERS
SAUTÉ OF KIDNEYS
SWEDISH MEATBALLS
STUFFED CABBAGE ROLLS
STUFFED ONION ROLLS
SWEDISH MEAT HASH
CREAMED SWEETBREADS
SWEDISH OMELET
SKÅNE POTATOES
POTATOES IN BÉCHAMEL SAUCE
CREAMED POTATOES
CHRISTMAS MUSTARD
RED CABBAGE

JANSSON'S TEMPTATION

This gratin dish is a classic constituent of the genuine Swedish smörgåsbord. "Jansson" is also an extremely popular late-night savory or "vickningsrätt", i.e. conclusion to a festive evening, when according to Swedish tradition the guests are offered something salty, an ice-cold snaps, good beer, crispbread and a generous slice or two of cheese in the small hours, before they leave.

> 6 medium-sized potatoes (raw)
> 2 onions
> 14–16 Swedish anchovy fillets
> 1 ½–2 dl (¾ cup) cream
> 2–3 tbsp breadcrumbs
> 2 tbsp butter for the dish

Peel the potatoes and shred them finely. Cut the onion into thin slices. Liberally butter an ovenproof dish with fairly high, vertical sides. Put a layer of potatoes in the bottom, followed by onion and then finely chopped Swedish anchovy fillets (preferably from canned whole anchovies) in rows, packed quite closely together. Repeat, finishing with potatoes.

Smooth out the surface and pour the cream on top, so that the potatoes may be glimpsed beneath. Dilute with liquid from the can. Finally, sprinkle fine breadcrumbs on top and bake in a moderately hot oven (200°C, 400°F) for about one hour.

Fried Swedish Anchovies or Smoked Baltic Herring

ANSJOVIS- ELLER BÖCKLINGFRÄS

Both these dishes may equally well be served as a first course, on fried bread or toast. The Swedish anchovy fillets should preferably – as in all Swedish anchovy recipes – come from whole anchovies, since they then taste substantially better.

> 1 large onion, very finely sliced
> 10–12 finely chopped Swedish
> anchovy or smoked Baltic herring fillets
> 4–5 hard-boiled, finely chopped eggs

Fry the onion in butter, adding the chopped anchovy or smoked herring together with the finely chopped eggs. Fry them all together rapidly in a hot pan. Season with freshly ground black pepper and serve at once.

This dish should never be placed on the smörgåsbord much in advance: if it has to stand, it loses its freshness.

Smoked Baltic Herring Casserole

BÖCKLINGLÅDA

Place fillets of smoked herring in a buttered baking dish on a bed of finely chopped dill. Sprinkle salt and pepper on top. Pour on enough thick cream barely to cover the fish. Bake in a medium-hot oven (about 200°C, 400°F) for 15–20 minutes, until the top is golden brown.

KAVIARSTRÖMMING

> 500 g (1 lb) Baltic herring
> 1 ½ tsp salted Swedish caviar
> 1 egg yolk
> 2 tsp chopped dill
> 1 tsp chopped chives
> 1 ½ dl (¾ cup) thick cream
> 2 tbsp butter for the dish

Clean the herring, removing the heads and bones. Spread out each herring, skin side down.

Mix the caviar, egg yolk, dill and chives. Lay a teaspoonful of the mixture on each of the spread-out fish. Roll up each herring, starting from the tail end, and place the rolls next to each other in a buttered ovenproof dish.

Blend the rest of the caviar mixture with the cream and pour it over the herring. Dot with butter, and bake in a moderately hot oven (200°C, 400°F) for about 20 minutes.

This dish may be served either hot or cold on the smörgåsbord. The cold version should form part of the second round.

When served with freshly boiled potatoes, Baltic herring with Swedish caviar is an excellent main dish.

HERRING PATTIES WITH CURRANT SAUCE

SILLBULLAR MED KORINTSÅS

This is an ancient Swedish dish, and a typical example of how people in one way and another sought to vary the eternal staple, salt herring. Here, the result of their efforts is an unqualified success.

> 1 large herring
> milk
> 300 g (1 cup) leftover fried or boiled
>   meat, preferably beef or veal

⅓ liter (1 ½ cups) cold boiled potatoes
1 red onion
white pepper
1 egg
1 level tsp potato flour
(thin cream)
butter for frying

Skin the herring, remove all bones and soak it in milk for several hours. Grind it finely with the meat, potatoes and onion (or use the blender). Mix in a little white pepper, the egg, potato flour and – if the mixture seems too stiff – a few tablespoonfuls of thin cream. Shape the forcemeat into small, flat patties and fry them in butter until they are golden brown. Serve with currant sauce (see below). If desired, the patties may be seasoned with finely chopped parsley.

Currant sauce is a sweet-sour accompaniment to herring patties, fried salt herring, fried salmon fins and boiled salt tongue.

2 tbsp currants
3 dl (1 ¼ cups) water
2 tbsp butter
2–3 tbsp plain flour
1–2 dl (¾ cup) stock
1 tbsp syrup
½ tbsp white spirit vinegar (12%)
Japanese soya sauce
butter
(salt)

Simmer the currants in water until soft. Strain, keeping the water. Make a roux of butter and flour, add the currant juice and stock, and simmer for 10 minutes. The sauce should be treacly, but not stiff. Add syrup and spirit vinegar to taste, until a sweet-sour flavor is achieved. Darken the sauce with a little Japanese soya sauce. Bring to a boil, add the currants and finish off with a dab of butter, and perhaps a little salt to taste.

SILLGRATÄNG

4 drained herring fillets
8 cold boiled potatoes, sliced
2 onions, thinly sliced
¾ dl (⅜ cup) breadcrumbs
2–3 tbsp butter

Sauté the onions gently in butter. Grease a shallow ovenproof dish liberally. Put slices of potato diagonally across the dish "à cheval", i.e. so that they overlap by half their diameter. Place a row of onion, followed by a row of herring fillet, on each side of the potato. Finish off with a row of potato on each side.

Sprinkle breadcrumbs and a little melted butter on top. Bake at 200°C (400°F) until the herring and onions are heated through and the top is an attractive golden brown color – about 25 minutes.

SILLGRATÄNG MED DILL

4 drained herring fillets
8 potatoes, peeled and thinly sliced
2 medium-sized onions, sliced
about 2 dl (¾ cup) thin cream
1 bay leaf
1 tsp thyme
white pepper
(salt)
1 bunch of dill, coarsely chopped
¾ dl (⅜ cup) breadcrumbs
1 dl (½ cup) grated cheese
2–3 tbsp butter

Boil the sliced potatoes and onions in the cream, with a tight-fitting lid on the saucepan, until they are soft. Season with crushed bay leaf, thyme, freshly ground white pepper and perhaps a little salt.

Grease a baking dish and put half the potatoes and onions in it. Sprinkle with half the chopped dill, and spread the herring fillets on top. Spread the remaining dill on the herring, and then cover with the rest of the potatoes and onions. Smooth down the surface and cover with a mixture of breadcrumbs and grated cheese. Pour a little melted butter on top, and bake in a hot oven (approx. 250°C, 500°F) for about 10 minutes, until the surface is an attractive golden brown color.

SALMON PUDDING

> 200 g (½ lb) salt salmon
> 750 g (2 lb) potatoes, boiled in their jackets
> 1 small onion
> 1 bunch of dill
> white pepper
> 4 dl (2 cups) thin cream
> 2 eggs
> butter for the dish

If the salmon is too salty, soak it in a little milk and water overnight.

Peel the cold boiled potatoes and cut them in slices. Finely chop the onion and dill. Wipe the salmon, cut it into small, thin slices and sprinkle them with pepper. Grease a deep ovenproof dish.

Alternate layers of potatoes and slices of salmon, sprinkling chopped dill and onion on each layer. The top and bottom layers should be potato. Whisk together the cream and egg, and pour the mixture on top. Dot with butter and bake in a moderate oven (approx. 175°C, 335°F) for 45–60 minutes.

Serve with melted butter.

HERRING PUDDING WITH POTATOES

SILLPUDDING MED POTATIS

Herring may be substituted for salmon in the above recipe. Alternate layers of boiled potatoes and shredded, drained herring fillets mixed with coarsely chopped dill in a well-greased oven dish. Pour on top the same egg and cream mixture as for salmon pudding. Bake in a medium-hot oven (200°C, 400°F) and serve with melted butter.

Fried Salmon Fins

This dish is quintessentially Swedish.

Take a side of smoked salmon and cut a thick strip of skin from the abdomen and grill bone towards the tail. Cut it into appropriately sized pieces. Dip the pieces in beaten egg and then in fine breadcrumbs, before frying them in a little butter or oil. When they are well browned, let them drain on kitchen paper before serving them in the hot section of the smörgåsbord.

Accompanied by currant sauce (see p. 85), pickled cucumber (see p. 78) and freshly boiled potatoes, these make a complete main dish in their own right.

Fried salmon fins may also be served cold on the smörgåsbord, in which case they belong in the second round.

Fried Baltic Herring Fillets

STRÖMMINGSFLUNDROR

1 kg (2 lb) Baltic herring
butter
chopped parsley
2–3 tsp salt
white pepper
¾ dl (⅜ cup) plain flour
1 egg
1 dl (½ cup) breadcrumbs
butter for frying

Clean and rinse the herring and drain them thoroughly. Remove the backbones and cut off the heads.

Mix the chopped parsley with the butter. Season the herring fillets with salt and pepper on the inside, and then put dabs of parsley butter on half of them. Put the buttered and non-buttered pieces together (skin side out) and dip the double fillets in plain flour seasoned with a little salt. Now dip them in beaten egg, and finally in breadcrumbs, well patted down so that they stick. Fry the herring rapidly in butter in a hot skillet.

OPERAKÄLLARENS STRÖMMING

Operakällaren ("the Opera cellar") is Sweden's best-known restaurant abroad, with a highly distinguished cuisine. Many foreign visitors to Stockholm have, over the years, savored the restaurant's magnificent smörgåsbord, which naturally includes a large number of dishes devised in Operakällaren's own kitchen. This Baltic herring dish is one of those.

1 kg (2 lb) fresh Baltic herring
2 egg yolks
2 dl (¾ cup) thick cream

FOR THE COATING:
1 ½ dl (¾ cup) rye meal
2–3 tsp salt

FOR THE FRYING:
2–3 tbsp margarine or butter

Clean and rinse the herring.

Whisk together the egg yolks and cream, and put the herrings in the mixture. Turn them several times so that they absorb as much as possible of the egg and cream; leave them for about an hour. Remove them and let them drain.

Reshape the herrings, coat them in rye meal mixed with salt. Fry them rapidly in a hot skillet, and serve immediately with boiled or puréed potatoes.

CHIMNEY SWEEPS

SOTARE

Take a quantity of absolutely fresh herring. Clean them, removing the heads but not the backbones. Heat a cast-iron skillet (preferably oiling it slightly first) until it is as hot as the hot-plate on a wood stove, and lay the herring in it side by side. The heat browns them quickly, almost burning them, on the outside.

Turn the fish and broil them rapidly on the other side. Remove and, after placing them on a hot dish, sprinkle them with very salty water and top them with a few pats of parsley or dill butter.

The best accompaniment to this dish is freshly boiled potatoes in their jackets.

FRESH EEL ROASTED ON RYE STRAW

HALMAD FÄRSK ÅL

Clean and skin a large eel and cut it in portion-sized chunks. Cover a baking dish with finely chopped, clean rye straw. Sprinkle salt, freshly ground black pepper and allspice over the pieces of eel, and place them – with the back uppermost – on the straw. Bake them in a hot oven (about 250°C, 500°F) until they are an attractive brown color; this usually takes about 20 minutes. During the roasting, a good deal of the eel's fat runs down into the straw, and the oven becomes filled with the smell and smoke from the slightly burnt straw, which contributes extra piquancy to the flavor of the delicious chunks of eel.

Serve the eel with lemon wedges, sharp sauce (see p. 61), sprigs of dill and freshly cooked new potatoes, or old ones squeezed through a press.

SALT SMOKED EEL

LUAD ÅL

Salt a medium-sized eel well and leave it to stand for about 6 hours. Clean and scrape it, but do not remove the skin. Rinse it thoroughly, and dry it well with a cloth. Put a layer of birchwood or alderwood embers and chopped juniper twigs in a baking pan, and place a rack on top. Put the eel on the rack, and place it in a very hot oven (about 250°C, 500°F). Roast the eel until its skin is dark brown and crusty, turning it several times during the roasting so that it is evenly colored all over.

Serve the eel whole and decorate it with lemon wedges and dill. Sharp sauce (see p. 61) and pressed potatoes, preferably with a pat of butter on top, go well with this dish.

SALTED EEL

RIMMAD ÅL

Clean, skin and bone an eel thoroughly. Cut it in 10 cm (4 inches) pieces and put the pieces in a dish, salting with 200 g (¾ cup) non-iodized salt (this should be somewhat coarse-grained and porous, e.g. sea salt). Cover with a plate and leave in a cool place for about 12 hours.

Remove the eel, rinse off the salt and pat dry with a towel. Salted eel may be prepared in many ways, e.g. boiled or grilled.

BOILED SALTED EEL

1 salted eel, cut in pieces
1 small onion, sliced
1 small carrot, sliced
1 bay leaf
¼ tsp thyme
10 white peppercorns

Bring to a boil 1 liter (2 pints) of water, containing the vegetables and seasoning. Leave to simmer for a while. Add the pieces of eel, and simmer for about 15 minutes. Remove the eel, drain it and serve it in a napkin with freshly boiled potatoes, or perhaps with puréed potatoes and a good sharp sauce (see p. 61) or Skåne mustard sauce.

GRILLED SALTED EEL

Brush the pieces of salted eel with oil and, using a peppermill, sprinkle a little pepper on top. Grill the pieces on a dry, smooth cast-iron skillet, after it has become really hot, until they are lightly browned all over. Chop some dill finely and stir it together with melted butter, a few drops of fresh lemon juice and perhaps a little freshly ground pepper.

Put the grilled eel on a dish, brush it with dill butter and serve the rest of the butter in a sauce bowl. Creamed potatoes, Skåne potatoes (see p. 104) or scrambled eggs are also good accompaniments.

JULKORV

1 kg (2 lb) lean fresh pork
1 kg (2 lb) beef
1 kg (2 lb) pork fat
1 kg (2 lb) boiled potatoes
3 tbsp salt
2 tsp ground white peppercorns
2 tsp ground allspice
1 tsp ground cloves
2 tsp ginger
2 tbsp potato flour
5 dl (2 cups) pork stock, made
   from boiled rind and bones
2 liters (4 pints) boiled milk
6 m (6 yards) sausage skin (or pig's
   intestines if available)

FOR RUBBING IN:
3 tbsp salt
2 tbsp sugar
1 ½ tsp saltpeter

FOR THE BRINE:
3 liters (6 pints) water
3 dl (1 ¼ cups) salt
½ tbsp sugar
½ tsp saltpeter

Grind the meat and pork fat three times, adding the cold potatoes the third time. Add the spices, ice-cold milk and stock; mix well, and knead the mixture thoroughly. Taste, and boil a small sample to check the seasoning.

Stuff the mixture very loosely into the well-washed intestines or sausage skin, tying at suitable intervals, and prick numerous very small holes in the skin so as to permit air to pass. Rub the sausages with a mixture of salt, sugar and saltpeter.

Put the sausages aside for a day and then put them in brine which has been boiled and thoroughly cooled. Keep the sausages in a cool place, but not for too long. If they remain in the brine for more than a week, they should be soaked in water for several hours before boiling.

When boiling the sausages, prick them all over with a darning needle, then put them in cold water with a couple of bay leaves, slices of onion, a few white peppercorns and some allspice. Bring slowly to a boil and simmer until the sausages are cooked right through, i.e. about 20 minutes.

VÄRMLAND SAUSAGE

VÄRMLANDSKORV

Värmland is a province in western Sweden, bordering on Norway. This farmhouse sausage originated there and has spread over the whole country with migrants from Värmland. At Christmas, it is often made at home; otherwise, it is available ready to eat.

> 500 g (1 lb) beef
> 500 g (1 lb) pork
> 200 g (6 oz) pork fat
> 1 ½ kg (3 lb) raw, peeled potatoes
> 1 medium-sized onion
> 1 ½ tbsp salt
> 2 tsp sugar
> 2 tsp white pepper
> 1 tsp allspice
> 2 ½ m (2 ½ yards) sausage skin (or pig's
> intestines if available)
> 2 dl (¾ cup) salt
> 1 tsp saltpeter
>
> FOR THE BRINE:
> 1 liter (2 pints) water
> 1 dl (½ cup) salt
> 2 tsp castor sugar

Dice half the pork fat finely. Grind the rest with the meat and potatoes as finely as possible (or use the blender). Add the seasoning and mix well. Check the flavor and consistency by frying a small amount. Stuff the sausage skin or well-washed intestines fairly loosely. Rub the sausage with a mixture of salt and saltpeter. Put it aside for 12–15 hours, and then put it in brine which has been boiled and thoroughly cooled. The sausage then becomes saltier. The sausage may be served hot or cold, cut in thick pieces, on the Christmas table or smörgåsbord.

FRIED PIG'S TROTTERS

GRILJERADE GRISFÖTTER

Prepare and cook the pig's trotters as in the recipe on p. 66, but do not place them in brine. Remove the large bones and place the trotters under pressure between two cutting boards with weights on top. Leave them to cool.

Toss the trotters in plain flour, dip them in beaten egg and finally roll them in breadcrumbs, patting the crumbs in well. Fry slowly in butter. Serve with pickled beets and mustard.

BOILED LAMB IN DILL SAUCE

KOKT LAMM I DILLSÅS

1 ½ kg (3 lb) breast and/or
  shoulder of lamb

FOR THE STOCK:
bones from the shoulder
¾ tbsp salt per liter (quart) of water
3–4 white peppercorns
1 leek
1 piece of carrot
dill stalks

FOR THE DILL SAUCE:
1 tbsp butter
2 tbsp plain flour
approx. 5 dl (2 cups) stock (in
  which the lamb has been cooked)
½ tbsp white spirit
  vinegar (12%) + 1 tbsp water
1 tbsp sugar
2 tbsp chopped dill
1 egg yolk
½ dl (¼ cup) thick cream

Divide the meat into suitable portion-sized pieces, rather small when it is to be served as a hot dish on the smörgåsbord, larger pieces when it is to be the main dish. Blanch by bringing to a boil in salted water and then immediately rinsing it in cold water. Put the meat and bones in a casserole and pour in fresh water so that the meat is barely covered. Bring to a boil, skim well and add the salt, pepper, leek, carrot and dill stalks. Simmer over a low heat until the meat is tender, i.e. 1–1 ½ hours. Transfer the pieces to a serving dish and keep it hot while you prepare the sauce.

Make a white roux with the flour and butter. Gradually add the strained hot stock. Simmer for 5 minutes. In the meantime, bring to a boil the spirit vinegar, water and castor sugar. Add this to the sauce until a sweet-sour flavor is obtained. Mix in generous quantities of coarsely chopped dill and whisk in the cream mixed with the egg yolk (the latter is optional). Pour the sauce over the meat, heat without boiling and serve hot with boiled potatoes.

SWEDISH BEEFBURGERS

BIFF À LA LINDSTRÖM

Theories differ as to who Lindström, the originator of this popular form of beef, really was, but most sources agree that he was a former Swedish consul in St. Petersburg, Henrik Lindström, who devised the dish more than a century ago at the table of the distinguished Hotel Witt in Kalmar, on Sweden's east coast. It is undoubtedly of Russian origin, like steak tartare.

400 g (1 lb) ground beef
2 dl (1 cup) water
2 eggs
3 tbsp capers
4 tbsp pickled beets, diced finely
3 tbsp finely chopped onion
1–1 ½ tsp salt
½ tsp freshly ground white pepper

Stir water and egg into the ground beef until it is pliant. Mix in the other ingredients.

Shape the mixture into fairly small, rounded patties and put them on a cutting board rinsed in water. Fry them immediately for 3–4 minutes on each side. The heat should be fairly high to begin with and then reduced. Remove, and lay the patties on a hot dish.

If the beefburgers are to be a main dinner dish, they may be accompanied by puréed or fried potatoes and shredded lettuce.

SAUTÉ OF KIDNEYS

NJURSAUTÉ

This smörgåsbord delicacy is best of all made from veal kidneys; failing that, pork or lamb kidneys may be used, but they must be soaked in cold water for several hours before the dish is prepared. Alternatively, one can blanch pork or lamb kidneys prior to preparing this dish.

> 500 g (1 lb) veal kidneys
> 200 g (1 cup) fresh mushrooms (or canned)
> 1 tsp plain flour
> ½ tsp salt
> ¼ tsp black pepper
> ½ dl (¼ cup) hot, strong stock
> 2–3 tsp dry madeira or sherry
> 2 tsp butter for frying
> finely chopped parsley

Clean the kidneys, removing membranes and all fat. Cut them in slices. Wash and slice the mushrooms.

Mix the flour, salt and pepper and toss the slices of kidney in the mixture.

Heat up the butter and brown the kidney slices rapidly on both sides. Put them aside, but keep them warm. Add more butter if necessary, turn down the heat and fry the mushrooms until they are golden brown.

Replace the kidneys in the pan. Add the stock and madeira or sherry and bring to a boil. Season well. Sprinkle finely chopped parsley on top and serve immediately.

As a main dish, braised kidneys are served with boiled rice and a green salad.

KÖTTBULLAR

"Nothing beats Mum's meatballs" – that's a proverb in Sweden. There's hardly anything more personal than a gourmet's meatball recipe, either. This is the author's version.

> 200 g (1 cup) boneless beef
> (without sinews and membranes)
> 100 g (½ cup) veal
> 100 g (½ cup) pork, preferably with
> fat (may be substituted by more beef)
> 1 dl (½ cup) crushed rusks or white bread
> 2 dl (¾ cup) cream
> ½ finely chopped onion
> 1 egg
> salt, white pepper
> butter for frying

Soak the bread in the cream. Grind the meat three or four times through the finest disc of the meat grinder, or use the blender. Add the cream and bread mixture for the last two times.

Brown the finely chopped onion a little in butter, stir it in with an egg and work the mixture until smooth. Add some water to give a smooth consistency, seasoning with pepper and salt as you go.

Fry a sample of two small balls in butter, until they are golden brown, to check the seasoning. When they taste good, it's time to start rolling the meat into balls. Put the balls on flat plates rinsed in cold water, or a wet cutting board.

For the smörgåsbord, you should make the meatballs walnut-sized; if they are to be a main dish, make them the size of ping-pong balls. The simplest method is to shape them using the wet palm of your hand and a couple of tablespoons, alternately standing them in a glass of hot water. Make all the balls even and neat before you start frying. Melt rather a large quantity of butter in a not-too-large frying pan and leave it to brown until it stops hissing. Then put in 10–20 meatballs at a time, depending on their size. Let them brown, and shake the pan now and again so that they roll round, removing each one as and when it is ready.

If the meatballs are to be served with gravy or sauce,

proceed as follows. Rinse the frying pan with water after each frying and add new butter, heating it up in the same way as the first time. When all the meatballs are ready, sprinkle a little plain flour in the pan, pour in the gravy (i.e. butter from the frying and water used to rinse the pan) and stir until the sauce is even. Flavor with a little white pepper, salt and perhaps some soya. Let the meatballs bubble gently for a few minutes in the sauce, over a low heat. If a creamy sauce is desired, pour thick or thin cream into the pan after the last frying.

Serve the meatballs with puréed potatoes, cowberry (or cranberry or red whortleberry) jam and salted or pickled cucumber. On the smörgåsbord, they may be served either cold, without sauce (in the third round) or hot, in the sauce (fourth round).

STUFFED CABBAGE ROLLS

KÅLDOLMAR

This dish, so beloved of Swedes, is a relic from an eighteenth-century war! It appeared in Swedish cuisine when Turkish creditors came to Sweden to collect the debts incurred by King Charles XII and his merry men in their country. Apparently, these Turks missed the stuffed vine leaves of their native country, and persuaded some lady in charge of the catering to make a Swedish version, replacing the vine leaves by cabbage leaves and the original lamb meat by beef and pork.

1 medium-sized white cabbage
150 g (¾ cup) ground beef
150 g (¾ cup) ground pork
½ dl (¼ cup) rice
1 ½ dl (¾ cup) milk for the rice
1 onion
2 eggs
1 ½ dl (¾ cup) milk (for the meat mixture)
salt, white pepper
2 tbsp syrup
3 tbsp butter
½ liter (2 cups) gravy or brown sauce

Discard the stalk and core of the cabbage head and place the cabbage in boiling salted water. Separate the leaves and cut away or slice up thinly the coarse central veins.

Rinse the rice and cook it in milk until all the liquid is absorbed and the rice is of a thick, porridge-like consistency. Chop the onion finely and brown it in butter. Add the onion, egg, milk, seasoning and the cold rice to the ground meat, and season to taste.

Place a generous tablespoonful of the mixture on each cabbage leaf and roll them up into small dolmas. Place them in a baking pan or casserole. Trickle a little syrup on top, together with some melted butter. Bake the stuffed cabbage rolls, turning them once, at about 225°C (435°F) for approx. 40 minutes.

Make a simple brown sauce as follows. Brown 2 tbsp plain flour in 1 tbsp butter. Dilute with cabbage liquid or stock and boil for 10 minutes. Season with salt, soya, a stock cube and pepper.

When the rolls have taken on a brown colour, the sauce is poured over them and the heat reduced to 200°C (400°F). Leave them to bubble gently in the sauce for about 30 minutes. Season the sauce to taste.

As a main dish, stuffed cabbage rolls are served with puréed or boiled potatoes.

STUFFED ONION ROLLS

LÖKDOLMAR

4–6 large onions
100 g (½ cup) ground veal
100 g (½ cup) ground pork
½ dl (¼ cup) water
½ dl (¼ cup) thick cream
2 tbsp breadcrumbs
salt
white pepper
1 tsp potato flour
soya sauce
butter for frying

Peel the onions and boil them in lightly salted water for 10 minutes. Leave them to cool, before the onion leaves separate.

Keep the water in which they were parboiled. Remove the inner part of the onion, chop it finely and add it to the ground meat. Mix together the water, cream, chopped onions and breadcrumbs and put aside for the breadcrumbs to absorb the liquid, for about 10 minutes. Then work the mixture, together with salt, pepper and potato flour, into the ground meat, and blend thoroughly. Season to taste.

Place a small amount of stuffing in each onion leaf, roll up and fasten with toothpicks, and then brown the onion rolls in butter. Put them in a greased baking dish and sprinkle with plain flour. Place in the oven (heated to about 225°C, 435°F) and let them take on a slightly deeper color. Pour on top about 1 dl (½ cup) of the water in which the onions were parboiled, flavored with a little soya. Braise them in the oven for about 30 minutes, and serve immediately on the smörgåsbord.

Stuffed onion rolls may also be served as a main dish, with a tasty potato purée.

SWEDISH MEAT HASH

PYTT I PANNA

The original Swedish meat hash is a typical way of using up leftovers. You take whatever you have and – at best – turn it into something really delicious. The potatoes may be either cooked or raw (raw is best), the ingredients can be more or less finely chopped (neither too large nor too small is best!) and so on. The ideal composition of the dish is as follows.

1 dl (½ cup) boiled salt brisket of beef, diced
1 dl (½ cup) boiled fresh brisket of beef,
    diced
1 dl (½ cup) roast veal or pork, diced
8 medium-sized, raw, peeled potatoes, diced
1 large onion, finely chopped
salt and white pepper to taste

All the ingredients except the onions should be cut into ½ cm (¼ inch) cubes. Start by frying the potatoes until golden brown and cooked through; add the onions, and then the meat. Continue the frying until the meat, too, becomes a bit crisp, but not dry. Season with salt and pepper.

The ingredients may also be fried one at a time – first the onions, then the potatoes, and finally the meat. When the meat is ready, the onions and potatoes are added to the mixture and rapidly heated up.

Swedish meat hash should preferably be served straight out of the frying pan, with fried eggs on top or raw egg yolks, in eggshell halves, alongside. Pickled beets and salted cucumber are the obvious accompaniments.

CREAMED SWEETBREADS

STUVAD KALVBRÄSS

850 g (2 lb) parboiled sweetbreads,
    cut into small pieces
1 large onion, chopped
8 cl (⅜ cup) sherry
2 tsp plain flour
2 ½ dl (1 cup) strong stock, well reduced
3 dl (1 ¼ cups) thick cream
1 tsp salt
1 tsp white pepper
1 tsp chopped parsley
2–3 tbsp butter for frying

Melt the butter in a frying pan and sauté the onion without coloring it. Add the sweetbreads and sauté them, also without browning them.

Pour the sherry over the sweetbreads and onion and let the liquid reduce completely. Sprinkle flour on top and mix well. Add the stock, stirring constantly. Cook for a few minutes. Add the cream, stirring all the time, and cook for a further 5–8 minutes. Season with salt and pepper.

Serve the creamed sweetbreads in a deep dish, decorated with chopped parsley. As a main dish, they are served with boiled rice.

SWEDISH OMELET

SVENSK OMELETT

4 dl (1 ¾ cups) milk
4 dl (1 ¾ cups) thin cream
4 eggs
1 egg yolk
1 level tbsp plain flour
1 tsp salt
butter

Bring the milk and cream to a boil. Whisk together the eggs and egg yolk and pour the hot milk mixture on top, whisking vigorously. Beat in the flour and salt. Bake in a buttered cast-iron pan at 200°C (400°F) for about 30 minutes, until the omelet has set and turned a light brown. Fold the omelet onto a serving platter and serve with some kind of creamed filling made of meat or fish, chicken, sweetbreads, spinach or asparagus.

SKÅNE POTATOES

SKÅNSK POTATIS

Peel and dice the potatoes and then fry them until light brown in butter or margarine, adding a little finely chopped onion towards the end. When the potatoes and onion have browned, pour a little creamy milk on top, and let the potatoes simmer until they are soft. Season with a little pepper and a dash of Japanese soya sauce, which provides both color and a mild salty taste.

POTATOES IN BÉCHAMEL SAUCE

STUVAD POTATIS

Make a good, smooth and not too thick béchamel sauce, using cream. Carefully stir in freshly boiled, peeled and sliced potatoes, while they are still hot. Season with salt and pepper. Fold in finely chopped dill or parsley, or both. Immediately before serving, sprinkle a few herbs on top.

CREAMED POTATOES

RÅSTUVAD POTATIS

Select potatoes of good quality, not floury in texture and preferably not new, and cook them very slowly in lightly salted creamy milk – just enough to cover the potatoes. They need no further attention, and when they feel sufficiently soft (not so soft that they fall apart) the sauce is rounded off with a dab of cold butter (stirred in until it melts) and sprinkled with dill, chives or parsley.

CHRISTMAS MUSTARD

JULSENAP

This mustard, served as an accompaniment to Yule ham, needs about a week in the refrigerator to reach its full flavor, and the longer it is kept the better it becomes. The wine vinegar gives sharpness and the syrup rounds it off, while the sour cream contributes a pungent touch.

1 dl (½ cup) mustard powder
1 ½ tbsp wine vinegar
1 tsp salt
1 tbsp light syrup
1 ½ dl (¾ cup) sour cream

Mix together the mustard powder, vinegar, salt and syrup until an even consistency is attained. Stir in the sour cream.
Pack the mustard into a suitable jar with a tight-fitting lid.

Red cabbage is common on the Christmas table in Sweden, particularly in the south, and also in neighbouring Denmark.

about 1 kg (2 lb) red cabbage
1 onion
4–5 hard cooking apples
6 whole cloves
2 tbsp sugar
2 tbsp wine vinegar
1 tsp salt
2 tbsp blackcurrant jelly
1 ½ dl (½ cup) red wine
2 tbsp butter for frying

Shred the red cabbage finely, cut the onion into chunks, core the apples and cut them into segments.

Melt the butter in a spacious, thick-bottomed saucepan. Place in it alternate layers of shredded cabbage, onion and apple, adding the spices, sugar, vinegar and salt a little at a time. Bring to a boil slowly, with the lid on, for 1 ½ hours. After about half the time, blackcurrant jelly and red wine are folded into the cabbage.

Red cabbage cooked in this way is served as an accompaniment to Yule ham, pork brawn, collared brawn and spare ribs.

BY NOW, our tour of the smörgåsbord is completed – almost. After all the salty, smoked and sometimes fatty food, we need something sweet and something fresh. Fruit salad – made of fresh fruit, varying according to the season – is no doubt the best way to finish the meal. The fruits used need not be anything out of the ordinary; whatever they are, they make a good salad. Avoid using canned fruit, however, with the exception of pineapple in its own juice, which is an excellent addition.

Something sweet also goes down well – for example, a cake served with the good strong coffee without which no Swedish meal is truly complete!

In this section, we have also included some highly typical Swedish desserts which can very well serve as the last course on the smörgåsbord.

FIFTH-ROUND DISHES

FRUIT SALAD
GOOSEBERRY COMPOTE
RHUBARB COMPOTE
PEARS IN COWBERRY SYRUP
PEARS WITH GINGER
PUNCH CAKE
KING OSCAR'S CAKE
CREAMED RICE
FRUIT MOUSSE
THIN PANCAKES
PANCAKE TORTE
APPLE CAKE WITH VANILLA SAUCE
SMÅLAND CHEESECAKE

FRUIT SALAD

Fruit salad is a good traditional Swedish dessert. The fruits it contains are, of course, grown in southern climes. The salad's composition varies according to season and availability of fresh fruit. Here is a classic mixture.

> 2 oranges
> 1 apple
> 1 banana
> 100 g (1 cup) grapes
> sugar to taste
> juice of ½ lemon

Peel the oranges, removing all the pith, and cut them in thin slices. Peel the apple and remove the core; cut it in small cubes. Slice the banana. Cut the grapes in half and remove the pips.

Place alternate layers of the fruit in a glass bowl, sprinkling a little sugar on each layer. Pour the lemon juice on top and chill the salad for several hours so that the juice accumulates. If desired, a few finely chopped almonds or walnuts may be sprinkled over the salad.

Serve with whipped cream.

GOOSEBERRY COMPOTE

KRUSBÄRSKOMPOTT

> 1 liter (4 cups) gooseberries
> 2 dl (¾ cup) water
> 1–2 dl (½–¾ cup) sugar

Top and tail the gooseberries. Bring the water and sugar to a boil. Add the berries and let them simmer until soft, i.e. 3–5 minutes.

The compote should be served cold with cream, a light sponge cake (for example, the cake base of punch cake) or an almond cake. It is also excellent with vanilla ice cream.

RABARBERKOMPOTT

Early, light-colored and crisp rhubarb should be used for this compote.

> 1 ½ liters (6 cups) rhubarb
> 1 ½ dl (¾ cup) sugar
> 2 ½ dl (1 cup) water
> peel of ½ lemon

Rinse the rhubarb stalks well, dry them and remove the thin outer membrane. Cut them in pieces about 6 cm (2 inches) long.

Bring the water and sugar to a boil. Shred the yellow part of half a lemon finely and add it to the sugar solution.

Carefully add enough rhubarb to cover the bottom, and let it simmer until almost soft. Remove it with a perforated ladle, transfer it to a serving dish and put another batch of rhubarb in to boil.

When all the rhubarb is cooked, strain the liquid over the rhubarb in the dish. Serve the compote cold with whipped cream and perhaps an almond cake.

PEARS IN COWBERRY SYRUP

Cowberries (or lingonberries) – the "red gold of the forest" as Swedes call them – grow in large quantities in the vast forests, and are similar to cranberries, although smaller and tastier. Pears in cowberry syrup are a popular dessert which is not difficult to make if you have access to small pears and to cowberries or cowberry syrup (cranberries may be used instead).

FOR EVERY POUND OF PEARS, USE:
½–¾ liter (1–1 ½ cups) sour cowberry syrup
500 g (1 cup) sugar

FOR THE COWBERRY SYRUP:
1 kg (2 cups) cowberries
5 dl (1 cup) water

Bring the berries to a boil, skim and let them simmer gently for about 10 minutes until they have lost their juice and become wrinkled. Strain through a cloth.

Rinse and peel the pears. Simmer them gently in the cowberry syrup, in which the sugar has been dissolved. The pears are ready when they are soft and translucent, i.e. after about 10 minutes.

Put the pears in small pots or glass jars. Bring the cooking liquid to a boil and skim well, then pour it over the pears. Place a small weight on top, so that the pears are kept submerged while they cool. Cover, and keep them in a cool place.

Serve cold with a bowl of whipped cream alongside.

INGEFÄRSPÄRON

1 kg (2 lb) hard "preserving pears"
500 g (2 cups) sugar
5 dl (2 cups) water
2–3 pieces of crushed root ginger

Peel the pears.

Mix the sugar, water and ginger and boil for several minutes. Add the peeled – but not cored – pears, and simmer them very gently in the liquid for about 3 hours. They should be soft and translucent.

Remove the pears and leave them to cool. Place them in jars and pour the strained cooking liquid on top. Keep them in a cool place.

Serve with thin or thick cream, the latter whipped until it is frothy.

PUNCH CAKE

PUNSCHTÅRTA

Strictly speaking, the traditional Swedish punch cake should
be square; but of course it tastes the same if baked in a round
mold. It is an easily made cake whose whole "personality"
stems from the punch. Swedish punch is a sweet and relatively
weak spirit beverage made of arrack, pure alcohol, water and
sugar. It is drunk extremely cold – except with yellow pea
soup, when it is served hot!

> 4 eggs
> 1 ½ dl (¾ cup) sugar
> ½ dl (¼ cup) plain flour
> ½ dl (¼ cup) potato flour
> ½ dl (¼ cup) punch or arrack essence
> butter and breadcrumbs for the mold
>
> FOR THE DECORATION:
> 2 dl (¾ cup) whipping cream, flavored with
> a few drops of punch

Whisk the eggs and sugar until fluffy. Mix in the flour and
pour the mixture into a well-greased square or round mold.
Bake in a medium-hot oven (about 200°C, 400°F) for 25–30
minutes. Test with a skewer to make sure that the cake is
cooked through.

Divide the cake into two when it has cooled, and sprinkle
the punch over both halves. Spread half the whipped cream
on one half, place the other on top and finish off with the rest
of the whipped cream.

The cake should be served well chilled.

OSCARSTÅRTA

A sweet, rich cake which is supposed to have been the favorite cake of King Oscar II of Sweden (1829–1907). It improves on being kept for a day in the refrigerator before serving.

FOR THE BASES:
150 g (1 ¼ cup) almonds
3 dl (1 cup) icing sugar
5 egg whites

FOR THE FILLING:
1 dl (½ cup) sugar
just under ½ cup water
3–4 egg yolks
200–225 g unsalted butter, at
    room temperature

FOR THE DECORATION:
1 pkt flaked almonds
icing sugar

Start by drawing 4 square or round bases on baking-sheet paper or buttered greaseproof paper.

Scald, peel and grind the almonds. Mix them with the sugar. Whisk the egg whites until they are stiff and fold them into the almond and sugar mixture. Spread out the cake dough on the four bases you have drawn; if you want each layer to be slightly thicker, you can make three bases instead.

Bake the bases in a cool oven (125°C, 240°F). Allow them to cool somewhat and then loosen them carefully from the paper.

Simmer the sugar and water to make the filling, continuing until the solution is well thickened and forms threads when you test it with a spoon. Whisk the egg yolks until they are fluffy, and pour the hot syrup into them, whisking vigorously all the time.

Beat the butter until it is soft, and then add the egg mixture (after it has cooled) gradually, stirring constantly. Continue stirring until the mixture is shiny, smooth and even.

Roast the almond flakes until they are an attractive golden brown color. Sandwich the layers of cake together with the filling, finishing with a thin layer of filling on top. Finally, sprinkle with icing sugar and decorate with almond flakes.

CREAMED RICE

RIS À LA MALTA

This dessert belongs primarily on the Christmas table but can also very well be set on a well-supplied smörgåsbord.

Boil round-grained rice until it is white, soft and dry; then mix in cream, whipped stiff and then flavored slightly with lemon, sugar and finely chopped fruit, such as pineapple, orange or fresh berries. Pack the creamed rice and fruit in a bowl, chill and then unmold on a dish.

Serve decorated with orange slices, pieces of pineapple or whole berries of the same kind as those used in the creamed rice.

FRUIT MOUSSE

TROLLMOS

Beat 4–6 egg whites until they are stiff. Fold in a fairly soft, slightly sweetened purée of gooseberries, rhubarb or apples. The mousse should be fairly sharp-tasting. These quantities make ½–¾ liter (1–1 ½ pints) of mousse, depending on how much fruit is used.

Serve well chilled with almond cakes or small macaroons.

TUNNA PANNKAKOR

A large proportion of the inhabitants of Sweden always eat thin pancakes with jam as a dessert on Thursdays – in spite of having yellow pea soup with pork as their filling main dish!

The pancakes should be thin and crisp, with a golden brown, lacy frill around the edge – this takes time and practice to achieve. By the time one has done so, one has presumably also arrived at the point at which the pancake batter can be made entirely "by feel". The main rule is that the quantity of liquid should be twice that of flour. The melted butter means that you don't have to grease the skillet every time.

2 eggs
3 dl (1 ¼ cups) plain flour
6 dl (2 ½ cups) milk
½ tsp salt
2 tbsp melted butter
(1 tsp sugar)

Beat the eggs with part of the flour until the mixture is smooth. Add more flour, stir and gradually dilute with milk. Stir in the salt and – just before cooking – the melted butter. Flavor with a little sugar, if desired, to taste. During the cooking, whisk the batter from time to time to prevent the flour sinking to the bottom.

Heat the frying pan slowly, with a little fat in it to begin with. Pour some batter in the middle of the pan, twist the pan carefully from side to side so that the batter spreads out evenly; when it is no longer liquid, turn the pancake using a spatula.

Put the pancakes on a dish, either rolled up or flat with strips of greaseproof paper between.

Serve with sugar or jam. The pancakes may also be used as crêpes, i.e. with various kinds of sweet or savory filling.

Pancake Torte

PANNKAKSTÅRTA

This is a glorified version of thin pancakes. To make the torte, lay the pancakes on top of each other with layers of smooth apple purée or fresh, slightly sweetened berries (blueberries, raspberries, sliced strawberries or whatever is available) between. Spread a generous layer of whipped cream on top.

Another version is made as follows. Prepare a light meringue mixture, using 2 egg whites and 4 tbsp sugar: beat until stiff and then spread it over and round the pile of pancakes. Place the torte in a hot oven (approx. 250°C, 500°F) until the meringue has turned an attractive golden brown color.

Butter a skillet or baking dish (with steep, fairly high sides) generously, and sprinkle a ½ cm (¼ inch) layer of breadcrumbs (some rye bread) mixed with a little sugar on the bottom and around the sides. Half-fill with peeled, cored apples cut in thinnish slices. Sprinkle with some more sugar – how much depends on the degree of sourness of the apples – and a little cinnamon. Place another layer of breadcrumbs mixed with sugar on top of the apple layer; spread another layer of apple slices on top, and finish with a generous layer of breadcrumbs and sugar. Dot liberally with butter.

Instead of the raw apple slices, one can use a fairly firm apple purée or compote, made by boiling cored but not peeled apples with a little water and sugar and flavoring with cinnamon.

Bake the cake at 200°C (400°F) until the breadcrumb topping has taken on an attractive golden brown color. Leave the cake to cool.

Loosen the cake from the edges with a knife. Try to shake it loose in the baking pan, and turn it out on a dish by holding the dish on top of the pan like a lid and rapidly inverting the pan; the whole cake should then be unmolded onto the dish.

If, however, you wish to serve the cake hot, it may remain in the baking pan.

Serve accompanied by home-made vanilla sauce.

3 dl (1 ¼ cups) thin cream
1 vanilla pod
3 egg yolks
2 tbsp sugar
2 dl (¾ cup) whipping cream

Bring the thin cream slowly to a boil with the chopped vanilla pod. (Do not use an aluminum saucepan, which becomes discolored.) Leave the saucepan, with its lid on, for about 15 minutes, so that the vanilla pod can impart its delicious flavor and aroma to the cream, and then remove the pod.

Mix the egg yolks and sugar, pour in a little hot vanilla cream – whisking continuously – and then pour the mixture into the saucepan. Still whisking, let the sauce simmer gently.

Put the saucepan in cold water and whisk until it cools. It should be light, porous and frothy. Finally, whip the cream and fold it in.

SMÅLAND CHEESECAKE

SMÅLÄNDSK OSTKAKA

Cheesecake (or curd cake, as it is perhaps more accurately termed) is a dish of ancient tradition in Swedish cuisine. Nowadays, it is usually bought ready to serve – but it is not particularly hard to make, providing you have a really large casserole.

Making cheesecake was an excellent means of using fresh milk in the days before universal dairies. Quite simply, you make fresh curd cheese from the milk, and use this for a cake. Exactly how this is done varies from one part of the country to another; the commonest is the sweet type of cheesecake, while the best-known is the version made in Småland (a large province in southern Sweden), containing a lot of cream and eggs, the recipe of which is given here.

12 liters (12–14 quarts) milk
6 tbsp plain flour
1 tbsp rennet
1 liter (1 quart) cream
6 eggs
3 ½ dl (1 ½ cups) sugar
100 g (¾ cup) sweet almonds
a few bitter almonds

Heat the milk very gently until it is lukewarm (37°C, 98°F), whisk in the flour and add the rennet. Stir the mixture until it thickens. Put it aside until it separates into curds and whey. Stir once more. The curds and whey should be fully separated.

Strain the mixture so that all the whey runs off and the quantity is considerably reduced.

Beat in the cream, eggs, sugar and blanched, peeled and ground almonds. Turn the mixture out into a well-buttered baking dish. Bake at about 175°C (335°F) for an hour and a half.

Serve with blackcurrant, strawberry or some other kind of jam, and whipped cream if desired.

Christmas is the most important Swedish holiday, gastronomically speaking: it is the occasion for many to set the great Christmas table, which is a special kind of old-fashioned smörgåsbord.

In olden times, each household slaughtered its pig in good time for Christmas. Then followed the arduous work of utilizing to the full the meat thus provided. Many parts of the animal became delicacies for the Christmas table: the Yule ham was steeped in sweetened brine, the head was turned into a hefty hunk of brawn, or else smoked and boiled whole, the trotters were scrubbed and scraped prior to salting, then boiled and ultimately mustard-glazed and grilled. The blood was used for black pudding, and the liver for pâté. Even the tail and ears were not wasted.

For foreigners, "Dip in the pot" is, no doubt, a remarkable dish. It is a relic from the days when the poor farm hands were invited to dip their bread in the broth in which the ham and jellied meats had been boiled – they certainly did not get a chance to help themselves to the meat.

The laborious tasks involved in dealing with the pig's carcase have now for the most part been taken over by slaughterhouses. We buy the ham ready-salted and often boned, so that all we have to do is to stick it in the pan and boil it. The pig's head, which formerly held pride of place in the middle of the Christmas table, with a ruddy apple in its snout, is now a rarity in private homes, though it may be found on a really well-supplied Christmas table at a restaurant. Many restaurants set up a Christmas table during December, and it has become fairly common to partake of the season's culinary delights in advance, sometime during the month.

The herring pickles still comprise the prelude to the buffet, as they do for the year-round smörgåsbord. Spiced herring (or Baltic herring), Swedish anchovies, glassblower's herring and pickled herring are, of course, present; and herring salad is an absolute must.

Here, too, is the lightly salted, boiled – and perhaps previously lightly smoked – Yule ham, deliciously mustard-glazed, the rind often decorated with a checkered pattern and a decorative carving fork adorning the bone. Pork brawn is, we can assume, made by boiling lean shoulder of pork. The trotters are a delectable sight – either jellied or grilled. The special Christmas sausage cannot be left out, and there is often some additional type of sausage such as smoked liver sausage, perhaps – or the typical country sausages of Värmland and Västergötland, in southwestern Sweden, now popular all over the country. Such sausages are, of course, homemade according to ancient recipes.

Collared brawn is also a suitable dish for the Christmas table, as is jellied veal, a bland, low-fat and welcome change from all the rich, strongly flavored dishes. Swedish Christmas food is in general highly spiced: cloves, ginger, allspice and bay leaves are classic ingredients of Swedish cuisine, especially at Christmas.

Mum's meatballs – prepared by a highly personal method, lovingly rolled and fried in butter at just the right temperature – are sure to be included too.

Another dish without which the Christmas table would not be complete is "lutfisk" (stockfish or ling –

salted, dried, split and submerged in a solution of slaked lime). In olden times, every household soaked its own dried fish (cod or coalfish) in a homemade lime solution. The dried fish had to be put in the solution on the 9th December in order to be sufficiently soaked and ready for cooking on Christmas Eve.

Lutfisk has an extremely unusual flavor and smell when it is prepared in the traditional Swedish way – it's a typical example of a speciality which one either loves or loathes. Traditionally, it is accompanied by boiled potatoes and béchamel sauce made of cream (or creamy milk) and strongly flavored with crushed black mustard seeds. Small, dried green peas are often boiled and served as a further accompaniment, as is coarsely ground allspice. Originally, "Russian peas" (dried in boxes heated over a fire and tasting, as a result, slightly smoked) were eaten with lutfisk.

As an accompaniment to the jellied meats and ham, some kind of cabbage is appropriate – red or white cabbage, or Brussels sprouts, prepared in slightly different ways in various parts of the country.

The final course – something sweet and something refreshing – is essential after the long, heavy meal. For example, a berry compote with Christmas crullers (a special kind of deep-fried biscuit) or almond mussels filled with raspberries and a little whipped cream; or of course a fresh fruit salad. "Spettekaka" – a cake baked on a wooden spit – is a noteworthy speciality of Skåne, consisting entirely of lightly sweetened meringue baked in a highly original way, which is another suitable constituent of the Christmas table.

DISHES PARTICULARLY SUITABLE FOR THE CHRISTMAS TABLE

DIP IN THE POT

DOPP I GRYTAN

The broth from the Yule ham, pork brawn and pork sausages may be mixed in a saucepan and boiled for a considerable length of time, so that it is reduced and becomes strong and tasty. Bear in mind the fact that the ham broth may be somewhat salty. Strain the broth well and season with a little ginger and a pinch of sage. Skim off the fat.

Serve the broth piping-hot with slices of wort-flavored bread (this is a *must*) to dip in the pot.

WORT-FLAVORED BREAD

VÖRTLIMPA

Wort-flavored bread is the foremost type of bread served on the Christmas table. It is baked with wort (the first stage in beer-making) as the liquid in the dough. The main function of this bread is to be dipped in broth. It is a sweetish and highly spiced bread.

> 3 liters (6 pints) wort
> 150 g (1 cup) fresh yeast
> 250 g (1 ½ cups) butter or margarine
> 3 dl (1 ¼ cups) syrup
> 2 tsp salt
> 1 tbsp ginger
> 1 tsp ground cloves
> peel of 6 Seville oranges, boiled and finely chopped
> 8 cups rye flour
> about 12 dl (5 cups) plain flour

Reduce the wort by boiling to 2 pints, preferably the day before the bread is to be baked.

Crumble the yeast in the mixing bowl, and stir in a little of the wort.

Melt the fat. Pour the wort and syrup on top and leave the mixture until it is lukewarm (37°C, 98°F).

Pour it over the yeast, and stir in the salt, peel, spices and about half the rye flour. Add the rest of the flour, alternating rye and plain flour and finishing with the latter. Work the dough until it is firm and smooth, cover it with a cloth and let it rise to double its bulk, i.e. for about 40 minutes.

Knead the dough well, first in the bowl and then on a lightly floured baking board, until it is smooth. Divide the dough into five parts and roll them out into five even, oblong loaves. Leave them to rise on a baking tray, after brushing the sides with a little fat so that they do not join together when rising. Prick them with a skewer, and bake them at about 175°C (335°F) for 50–60 minutes.

Brush the loaves with hot water several times during the baking, and when they are finished. Leave them to cool covered with a cloth.

SAFFRON BREAD

SAFFRANSBRÖD

This bread is baked in the vast majority of Swedish homes at Christmas. Traditionally, the first saffron bread of the year is eaten on St. Lucia's Day, 13 December.

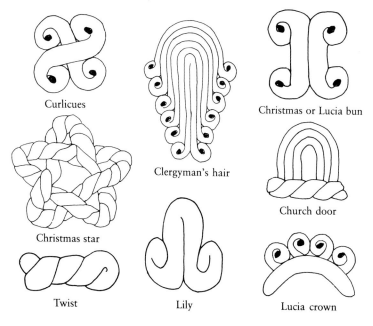

Curlicues

Clergyman's hair

Christmas or Lucia bun

Christmas star

Church door

Twist

Lily

Lucia crown

The bread is baked in the form of plaits or wreaths, but best of all as special Christmas buns or "kusar", which may be in the shape of lilies, figures-of-eight, sheaves and "lussekatter" (flat rolls with a currant at each of the four rounded corners), or of some religious motif – anything from priests'and angels' "hair" (like pretzels) to twelve-hole twists or church doors The guiding principle is to roll out pieces of dough the thickness of a finger, and then twist them, or put two or more together, in various artistic ways.

The quantities given here are enough for 3–4 large plaits, 2–3 wreaths or about 30 buns.

1–1 ½ g (1 pinch) saffron
50 g (¼ cup) fresh yeast
½ liter (2 cups) milk
1 egg
150–200 g (1 cup) butter or margarine
½ tsp salt
2–3 dl (1 cup) sugar
1 ½ liters (12–14 cups) plain flour

FLAVORING (OPTIONAL):
1 dl (½ cup) peeled, chopped sweet almonds
or
1 ½ dl (¾ cup) raisins
or
1 dl (½ cup) chopped candied peel

BRUSH AND DECORATE WITH:
1 egg
crystallized sugar
chopped almonds or raisins

Crush the saffron with a lump of sugar.

Crumble the yeast in a mixing bowl, and mix in a few tablespoonfuls of milk. Stir in the egg.

Melt the fat. Pour the milk on top and leave it until it is lukewarm (37°C, 98°F). Add the saffron.

Pour the milk over the yeast and stir in the salt, sugar, about half the flour and the extra flavoring, if desired. Add the rest of the flour one spoonful at a time, and work the dough until it is smooth, firm and shiny. Sprinkle a little flour on top, cover with a cloth and leave the dough to rise until it has doubled its bulk.

Work the dough down again in the bowl, then transfer it to a lightly floured baking board and knead it until smooth. Divide the dough and shape it into plaits, wreaths, small buns or rolls.

Put the shaped bread on buttered baking dishes and leave it to rise. Brush with egg and sprinkle with sugar and almonds, or decorate solely with raisins.

Bake the plaits and wreaths at 200°C (400°F) for 20–25 minutes, and the Christmas buns and rolls at 225°C (430°F) for about 10 minutes.

CHRISTMAS CRULLERS

KLENÄTER

These are a very special kind of Swedish cookie, traditionally baked for Christmas. They are an excellent accompaniment to berries (such as cloudberries, which grow in the north of Sweden) or fruit desserts.

5 egg yolks
50 g (½ cup) sugar
50 g (½ cup) melted butter
200 g (2 cups) plain flour
grated peel of ½ lemon
1 tbsp brandy
oil for frying

Beat the egg yolks and sugar until pale and frothy. Mix in the other ingredients to form a fairly soft dough. Leave it in the refrigerator for a few hours.

Roll out the dough thinly (about 2–3 mm, ⅛ inch) and cut out strips about 2 cm (¾ inch) wide. Now cut these strips at an angle (preferably with a pastry cutter which leaves the edges fluted) into pieces about 10 cm (4 inches) long. Finally cut a lengthwise slit in the middle of each piece, and pull one end of each strip through the slit to form a half-bow.

Deep-fry the crullers until they are a light golden brown, in fat or oil that is not too hot. Drain them thoroughly on kitchen paper. Before serving, they may be tossed gently in castor sugar.

GINGER COOKIES

PEPPARKAKOR

These quantities make about 300 ginger cookies.

3 dl (1 ¼ cups) brown sugar (e.g. demerara)
2 ½ dl (1 cup) castor sugar
½ dl (¾ cup) syrup
½ dl (¾ cup) water
300 g (1 ¼ cups) butter or margarine
1 tbsp cinnamon
1 tbsp ginger
1 tbsp bicarbonate of soda
1 ½ liters (12–14 cups) plain flour

Bring to a boil the brown and castor sugar, syrup and water. Add the fat and let it melt, then put the mixture aside to cool.

Stir in the spices, bicarbonate of soda and most of the flour. Cover the dough with the rest of the flour and chill, preferably until the next day.

Work the dough smooth on the baking board. Roll it out thinly, a little at a time (about 2 mm, ⅛ inch). Cut the cakes out with shaped cutters, and place them on a buttered baking tray. Bake at about 175°C (335°F) for 8–10 minutes. Leave them to cool on the baking tray.

APPROXIMATE CONVERSION TABLES

LIQUID MEASURES

American	British	Continental
1 tbsp (= 3 tsp)	1 dessertspoon	15 ml
⅛ cup	1 fl oz	25 ml
¼ cup	2 fl oz	50 ml (5 cl)
⅜ cup	3 fl oz	75 ml
½ cup	4 fl oz	1 dl
¾ cup	6 fl oz	1½–2 dl
1 cup (½ pint)	8 fl oz	2½ dl
1¼ cups	½ pint (10 fl oz)	3 dl
1½ cups	12 fl oz	3½ dl
1¾ cups	14 fl oz	4 dl
2 cups (1 pint)	16 fl oz	4½ dl
2½ cups	1 pint (20 fl oz)	6 dl
2 pints	a little > 1 ½ pints	a little < 1 liter

WEIGHTS

Butter:		
1 tbsp	½ oz	15 g
1 cup	8 oz	225 g
Flour:		
2 tbsp	½ oz	15 g
¼ cup	1 oz	30 g
4 cups	1 lb	450 g
Castor sugar:		
2 tbsp	1 oz	30 g
1 cup	8 oz	225 g
2 cups	1 lb	450 g
Gelatin:		
1 tbsp	¼ oz	2½ leaves/10 g
1 envelope	¾ tbsp	3 leaves/12 g

OVEN TEMPERATURES

	Fahrenheit	Gas mark	Celsius
Very slow or cool	225	¼	110
	250	½	130
Slow or cool	275	1	140
	300	2	150
Very moderate	325	3	170
Moderate	350	4	180
Moderately hot	375	5	190
	400	6	200
Hot	425	7	220
	450	8	230
Very hot	475	9	240
	500	10	250

INDEX